GILBERT
WITHOUT
SULLIVAN

A STUDIO BOOK

The Viking Press
New York

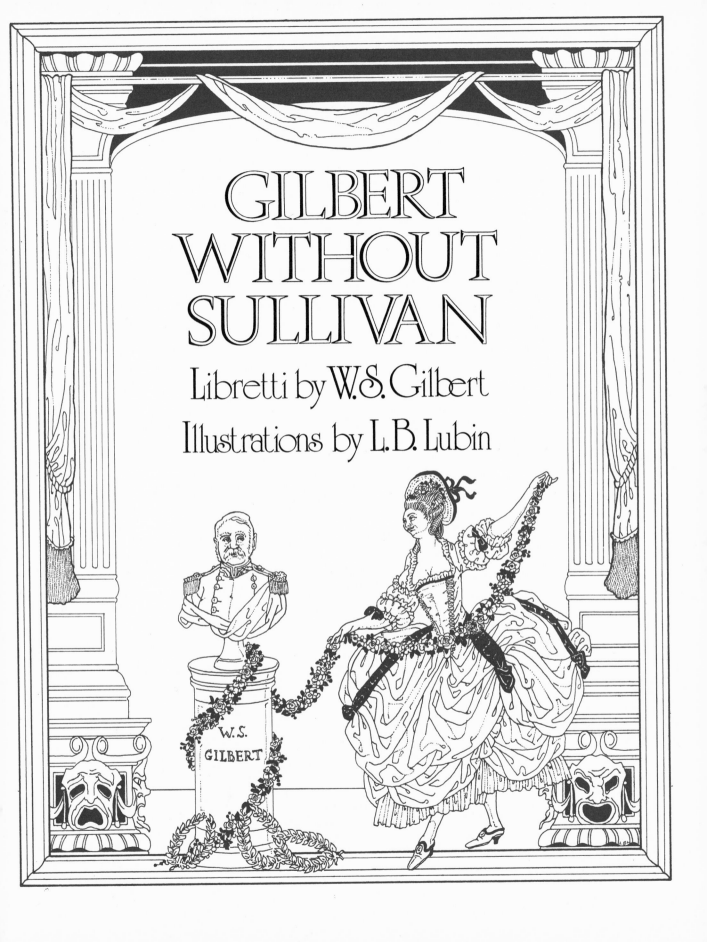

GILBERT WITHOUT SULLIVAN

Libretti by W.S. Gilbert

Illustrations by L.B. Lubin

First published in 1981 by The Viking Press (A Studio Book)
625 Madison Avenue, New York, N.Y. 10022
Published simultaneously in Canada by
Penguin Books Canada Limited

Library of Congress Cataloging in Publication Data
Sullivan, Arthur, Sir, 1842–1900.
[Operas. Librettos. Selections]
Gilbert without Sullivan.
(A Studio book)
Contents: The pirates of Penzance–H.M.S.
Pinafore–The Mikado–The gondoliers.
1. Operas–Librettos.   I. Gilbert, W. S.
(William Schwenck), 1836–1911.   II. Lubin,
Leonard B.   III. Title.
ML49.S9V5   782.81'2   81-43017
        ISBN 0-670-34010-3   AACR2

Printed in the United States of America
Set in Garamond

Contents

To Scott Shade and Nils Roest

ProloguE

William Schwenck Gilbert, the dramatist, and Arthur Seymour Sullivan, the composer, began their long—and often conflict-fraught—collaboration in December of 1871 with their "short burlesque" *Thespis;* a quarter of a century later, in March of 1896, their partnership ended with *The Grand Duke.* During those years Gilbert and Sullivan created fourteen light operas that together convey a nostalgic sense of the Victorian Englishman and his world better than any other works of art produced during the same period.

Sullivan was a composer of some renown when he and Gilbert first met. Throughout their collaboration he became increasingly dissatisfied with what he saw as his role as subordinate to the rather high-handed and demanding Gilbert. Sullivan considered his music to be of a higher caliber than the "silly" lyrics connected with it.

Gilbert, a veritable treasure trove of ideas and experiences, often based his complex plots on the nucleus of some personal encounter. His plots twist and turn; lovers separate and then reunite; beggars become kings (and kings sometimes beggars); virtue triumphs over all; and inevitably everybody and everything reach a satisfactory conclusion. A man of firm opinions, Gilbert became thoroughly involved with the details pertaining to the production of the operettas, extending his artistic control not only to the sets and costumes that were used but also to the staging and the very gestures that the characters were to employ.

In spite of their sometimes bitter differences, it has often been said that the marriage of Gilbert's words and Sullivan's music has never been equaled in the history of musical theater.

The full libretti–today's "standard versions"–of four of their most popular operettas are included in this book: *H.M.S. Pinafore,* first performed in London, at the Opéra Comique, in May of 1878; *The Pirates of Penzance,* produced initially in New York, in December of 1879, and then in London, at the Opéra Comique, in April of 1880; *The Mikado,* first staged at the Savoy Theatre, in London, in March of 1885; and *The Gondoliers,* which opened at the Savoy in December of 1889. Their other operas are *Trial by Jury* (1875), *The Sorcerer* (1877), *Patience* (1881), *Iolanthe* (1882), *Princess Ida* (1884), *Ruddigore* (1887), *The Yeoman of the Guard* (1888), *Utopia Limited* (1893), and, of course, *The Grand Duke* (1896).

The ingenious, topical lyrics and the bouncy, tongue-in-cheek music appeal greatly to my sense of fun. They conjure up a fabulous bygone era, entrancing us with a world of wit that will forever be peopled by extremely colorful prototypes playing out their rather self-centered roles. While much of the satire pertains to events, people, and ideas connected with the Victorian period, the charm of the verse shines through as brilliantly today as it did when audiences were first introduced to the operas a century ago.

It was no easy task for me to choose the particular verses that I would illustrate. Often a word or two, a phrase, or a concept jumped off the page and demanded visual interpretation. Occasionally one of the often pompous characters or absurd situations simply "tickled my fancy."

I hope that my illustrations have captured some of the charm, humor, and "sensible" nonsense permeating these delightful operas. My only regret is that it is not possible to convey through drawings the sparkling quality that Gilbert's words attain when they are coupled with Sullivan's enchanting music. This can be fully realized only when one has the good fortune to attend a performance of a Gilbert and Sullivan opera.

H.M.S. PINAFORE

DRAMATIS PERSONÆ

THE RT. HON. SIR JOSEPH PORTER, K.C.B. (*First Lord of the Admiralty*).

CAPTAIN CORCORAN (*Commanding H.M.S.* Pinafore).

TOM TUCKER (*Midshipmite*).

RALPH RACKSTRAW (*Able Seaman*).

DICK DEADEYE (*Able Seaman*).

BILL BOBSTAY (*Boatswain's Mate*).

BOB BECKET (*Carpenter's Mate*).

JOSEPHINE (*the Captain's Daughter*).

HEBE (*Sir Joseph's First Cousin*).

MRS. CRIPPS (LITTLE BUTTERCUP) (*a Portsmouth Bumboat Woman*).

First Lord's Sisters, his Cousins, his Aunts, Sailors, Marines, etc.

Scene: QUARTER-DECK OF H.M.S. *Pinafore*, OFF PORTSMOUTH.

ACT I.–*Noon.*　　　ACT II.–*Night.*

First produced at the Opéra Comique on May 25, 1878

H.M.S. PINAFORE
OR, THE LASS THAT LOVED A SAILOR

ACT I

SCENE—*Quarter-deck of H.M.S.* Pinafore. *Sailors, led by* BOAT-SWAIN, *discovered cleaning brasswork, splicing rope, etc.*

CHORUS

We sail the ocean blue,
And our saucy ship's a beauty;
We're sober men and true,
And attentive to our duty.
When the balls whistle free
O'er the bright blue sea,
We stand to our guns all day;
When at anchor we ride
On the Portsmouth tide,
We have plenty of time to play.

Enter LITTLE BUTTERCUP, *with large basket on her arm*

RECITATIVE—BUTTERCUP

Hail, men-o'-war's men—safeguards of your nation,
Here is an end, at last, of all privation;
You've got your play—spare all you can afford
To welcome Little Buttercup on board.

ARIA—BUTTERCUP

For I'm called Little Buttercup—dear Little Buttercup,
  Though I could never tell why,
But still I'm called Buttercup—poor little Buttercup,
  Sweet Little Buttercup I!

I've snuff and tobaccy, and excellent jacky,
  I've scissors, and watches, and knives;
I've ribbons and laces to set off the faces
  Of pretty young sweethearts and wives.

I've treacle and toffee, I've tea and I've coffee,
  Soft tommy and succulent chops;
I've chickens and conies, and pretty polonies,
  And excellent peppermint drops.

Then buy of your Buttercup—dear Little Buttercup;
  Sailors should never be shy;
So, buy of your Buttercup—poor Little Buttercup;
  Come, of your Buttercup buy!

BOAT. Aye, Little Buttercup—and well called—for you're the rosiest, the roundest, and the reddest beauty in all Spithead.

BUT. Red, am I? and round—and rosy! Maybe, for I have dissembled well! But hark ye, my merry friend—hast ever thought that beneath a gay and frivolous exterior there may lurk a canker-worm which is slowly but surely eating its way into one's very heart?

BOAT. No, my lass, I can't say I've ever thought that.

Enter DICK DEADEYE. *He pushes through sailors, and comes down*

DICK. *I* have thought it often. (*All recoil from him.*)

BUT. Yes, you look like it! What's the matter with the man? Isn't he well?

BOAT. Don't take no heed of *him;* that's only poor Dick Deadeye.

DICK. I say—it's a beast of a name, ain't it—Dick Deadeye?

BUT. It's not a nice name.

DICK. I'm ugly too, ain't I?

BUT. You are certainly plain.

DICK. And I'm three-cornered too, ain't I?

BUT. You are rather triangular.

DICK. Ha! ha! That's it. I'm ugly, and they hate me for it; for you all hate me, don't you?

ALL. We do!

DICK. There!

BOAT. Well, Dick, we wouldn't go for to hurt any fellow-creature's feelings, but you can't expect a chap with such a name as Dick Deadeye to be a popular character—now can you?

DICK. No.

BOAT. It's asking too much, ain't it?

DICK. It is. From such a face and form as mine the noblest sentiments sound like the black utterances of a depraved imagination. It is human nature—I am resigned.

RECITATIVE—BUTTERCUP *and* BOATSWAIN

BUT. (*looking down hatchway*).
    But, tell me—who's the youth whose faltering feet
        With difficulty bear him on his course?
BOAT. That is the smartest lad in all the fleet—
        Ralph Rackstraw!
BUT. Ha! That name! Remorse! remorse!

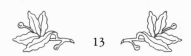

Enter RALPH *from hatchway*

MADRIGAL—RALPH

The Nightingale
Sighed for the moon's bright ray,
And told his tale
In his own melodious way!
He sang "Ah, well-a-day!"

ALL.   He sang "Ah, well-a-day!"

The lowly vale
For the mountain vainly sighed,
To his humble wail
The echoing hills replied.
They sang "Ah, well-a-day!"

ALL.   They sang "Ah, well-a-day!"

RECITATIVE—RALPH

I know the value of a kindly chorus,
But choruses yield little consolation
When we have pain and sorrow too before us!
I love—and love, alas, above my station!

BUT. (*aside*). He loves—and loves a lass above his station!
ALL. (*aside*). Yes, yes, the lass is much above his station!
                              [*Exit* LITTLE BUTTERCUP.

BALLAD—RALPH

A maiden fair to see,
The pearl of minstrelsy,
    A bud of blushing beauty;
For whom proud nobles sigh,
And with each other vie
    To do her menial's duty.

ALL.   To do her menial's duty.

A suitor, lowly born,
With hopeless passion torn,
    And poor beyond denying,
Has dared for her to pine
At whose exalted shrine
    A world of wealth is sighing.

ALL.   A world of wealth is sighing.

Unlearned he in aught
Save that which love has taught
    (For love had been his tutor);
Oh, pity, pity me—
Our captain's daughter she,
    And I that lowly suitor!

ALL.   And he that lowly suitor!

BOAT. Ah, my poor lad, you've climbed too high: our worthy captain's child won't have nothin' to say to a poor chap like you. Will she, lads?

ALL. No, no.
DICK. No, no, captains' daughters don't marry foremast hands.
ALL. (*recoiling from him*). Shame! shame!
BOAT. Dick Deadeye, them sentiments o' yourn are a disgrace to our common natur'.
RALPH. But it's a strange anomaly, that the daughter of a man who hails from the quarter-deck may not love another who lays out on the fore-yard arm. For a man is but a man, whether he hoists a flag at the main-truck or his slacks on the main-deck.
DICK. Ah, it's a queer world!
RALPH. Dick Deadeye, I have no desire to press hardly on you, but such a revolutionary sentiment is enough to make an honest sailor shudder.
BOAT. My lads, our gallant captain has come on deck; let us greet him as so brave an officer and so gallant a seaman deserves.

Enter CAPTAIN CORCORAN

RECITATIVE—CAPTAIN *with* CREW

CAPT. My gallant crew, good morning.
ALL (*saluting*). Sir, good morning!
CAPT. I hope you're all quite well.
ALL (*as before*). Quite well; and you, sir?
CAPT. I am in reasonable health, and happy
            To meet you all once more.
ALL (*as before*). You do us proud, sir!

SONG—CAPTAIN

CAPT.   I am the Captain of the *Pinafore;*
ALL.   And a right good captain, too!
CAPT.   You're very, very good,
            And be it understood,
        I command a right good crew.
ALL.   We're very, very good,
            And be it understood,
        He commands a right good crew.
CAPT.   Though related to a peer,
        I can hand, reef, and steer,
            And ship a selvagee;
        I am never known to quail
        At the fury of a gale,
            And I'm never, never sick at sea!
ALL.   What, never?
CAPT.   No, never!
ALL.   What, *never?*
CAPT.   Hardly ever!
ALL.   He's hardly ever sick at sea!
        Then give three cheers, and one cheer more,
        For the hardy Captain of the *Pinafore!*

CAPT.   I do my best to satisfy you all—
ALL.   And with you we're quite content.
CAPT.   You're exceedingly polite,

I've snuff and tobaccy, and excellent jacky, . . .

And I think it only right
To return the compliment.

ALL. We're exceedingly polite,
And he thinks it's only right
To return the compliment.

CAPT. Bad language or abuse,
I never, never use
Whatever the emergency;
Though "Bother it" I may
Occasionally say,
I never use a big, big D—

ALL. What, never?

CAPT. No, never!

ALL. What, *never?*

CAPT. Hardly ever!

ALL. Hardly ever swears a big, big D—
Then give three cheers, and one cheer more,
For the well-bred Captain of the *Pinafore!*

[*After song exeunt all but* CAPTAIN.

Enter LITTLE BUTTERCUP

RECITATIVE—BUTTERCUP *and* CAPTAIN

BUT. Sir, you are sad! The silent eloquence
Of yonder tear that trembles on your eyelash
Proclaims a sorrow far more deep than common;
Confide in me—fear not—I am a mother!

CAPT. Yes, Little Buttercup, I'm sad and sorry—
My daughter, Josephine, the fairest flower
That ever blossomed on ancestral timber,
Is sought in marriage by Sir Joseph Porter,
Our Admiralty's First Lord, but for some reason
She does not seem to tackle kindly to it.

BUT. (*with emotion*). Ah, poor Sir Joseph! Ah, I know too well
The anguish of a heart that loves but vainly!
But see, here comes your most attractive daughter.
I go—Farewell!
[*Exit.*

CAPT. (*looking after her*). A plump and pleasing person!
[*Exit.*

Enter JOSEPHINE, *twining some flowers which she carries in a small basket*

BALLAD—JOSEPHINE

Sorry her lot who loves too well,
Heavy the heart that hopes but vainly,
Sad are the sighs that own the spell,
Uttered by eyes that speak too plainly;
Heavy the sorrow that bows the head
When love is alive and hope is dead!

Sad is the hour when sets the sun—
Dark is the night to earth's poor daughters,
When to the ark the wearied one

Flies from the empty waste of waters!
Heavy the sorrow that bows the head
When love is alive and hope is dead!

Enter CAPTAIN

CAPT. My child, I grieve to see that you are a prey to melancholy. You should look your best to-day, for Sir Joseph Porter, K.C.B., will be here this afternoon to claim your promised hand.

JOS. Ah, father, your words cut me to the quick. I can esteem—reverence—venerate Sir Joseph, for he is a great and good man; but oh, I cannot love him! My heart is already given.

CAPT. (*aside*). It is then as I feared. (*Aloud.*) Given? And to whom? Not to some gilded lordling?

JOS. No, father—the object of my love is no lordling. Oh, pity me, for he is but a humble sailor on board your own ship!

CAPT. Impossible!

JOS. Yes, it is true—too true.

CAPT. A common sailor? Oh fie!

JOS. I blush for the weakness that allows me to cherish such a passion. I hate myself when I think of the depth to which I have stooped in permitting myself to think tenderly of one so ignobly born, but I love him! I love him! I love him! (*Weeps.*)

CAPT. Come, my child, let us talk this over. In a matter of the heart I would not coerce my daughter—I attach but little value to rank or wealth, but the line must be drawn somewhere. A man in that station may be brave and worthy, but at every step he would commit solecisms that society would never pardon.

JOS. Oh, I have thought of this night and day. But fear not, father, I have a heart, and therefore I love; but I am your daughter, and therefore I am proud. Though I carry my love with me to the tomb, he shall never, never know it.

CAPT. You *are* my daughter after all. But see, Sir Joseph's barge approaches, manned by twelve trusty oarsmen and accompanied by the admiring crowd of sisters, cousins, and aunts that attend him wherever he goes. Retire, my daughter, to your cabin—take this, his photograph, with you—it may help to bring you to a more reasonable frame of mind.

JOS. My own thoughtful father!

[*Exit* JOSEPHINE. CAPTAIN *remains and ascends the poop-deck.*

BARCAROLLE (*invisible*)

Over the bright blue sea
Comes Sir Joseph Porter, K.C.B.,
Wherever he may go
Bang-bang the loud nine-pounders go!
Shout o'er the bright blue sea
For Sir Joseph Porter, K.C.B.

[*During this the Crew have entered on tiptoe, listening attentively to the song.*

CHORUS OF SAILORS

Sir Joseph's barge is seen,
    And its crowd of blushing beauties,
We hope he'll find us clean,
    And attentive to our duties.
We sail, we sail the ocean blue,
    And our saucy ship's a beauty.
We're sober, sober men and true
    And attentive to our duty.
We're smart and sober men,
    And quite devoid of fe-ar,
In all the Royal N.
    None are so smart as we are.

Enter SIR JOSEPH'S FEMALE RELATIVES

(*They dance round stage*)

REL.   Gaily tripping,
        Lightly skipping,
    Flock the maidens to the shipping.
SAILORS. Flags and guns and pennants dipping!
    All the ladies love the shipping.
REL.   Sailors sprightly
        Always rightly
    Welcome ladies so politely.
SAILORS. Ladies who can smile so brightly,
    Sailors welcome most politely.
CAPT. (*from poop*). Now give three cheers, I'll lead the way.
ALL.   Hurrah! hurrah! hurrah! hurray!

Enter SIR JOSEPH *with* COUSIN HEBE

SONG—SIR JOSEPH

    I am the monarch of the sea,
        The ruler of the Queen's Navee,
    Whose praise Great Britain loudly chants.
COUSIN HEBE.   And we are his sisters, and his cousins,
        and his aunts!
REL.   And we are his sisters, and his cousins, and
        his aunts!
SIR JOSEPH. When at anchor here I ride,
        My bosom swells with pride,
    And I snap my fingers at a foeman's taunts;
COUSIN HEBE.   And so do his sisters, and his cousins, and
        his aunts!
ALL.   And so do his sisters, and his cousins, and
        his aunts!
SIR JOSEPH. But when the breezes blow,
        I generally go below,
    And seek the seclusion that a cabin grants;
COUSIN HEBE.   And so do his sisters, and his cousins, and
        his aunts!
ALL.   And so do his sisters, and his cousins, and
        his aunts!
    His sisters and his cousins,
    Whom he reckons up by dozens,
        And his aunts!

SONG—SIR JOSEPH

When I was a lad I served a term
As office boy to an Attorney's firm.
I cleaned the windows and I swept the floor,
And I polished up the handle of the big front door.
    I polished up that handle so carefullee
    That now I am the Ruler of the Queen's Navee!

CHORUS.—He polished, etc.

As office boy I made such a mark
That they gave me the post of a junior clerk.
I served the writs with a smile so bland,
And I copied all the letters in a big round hand—
    I copied all the letters in a hand so free,
    That now I am the Ruler of the Queen's Navee!

CHORUS.—He copied, etc.

In serving writs I made such a name
That an articled clerk I soon became;
I wore clean collars and a brand-new suit
For the pass examination at the Institute.
    And that pass examination did so well for me,
    That now I am the Ruler of the Queen's Navee!

CHORUS.—And that pass examination, etc.

Of legal knowledge I acquired such a grip
That they took me into the partnership.
And that junior partnership, I ween,
Was the only ship that I ever had seen.
    But that kind of ship so suited me,
    That now I am the Ruler of the Queen's Navee!

CHORUS.—But that kind, etc.

I grew so rich that I was sent
By a pocket borough into Parliament.
I always voted at my party's call,
And I never thought of thinking for myself at all.
    I thought so little, they rewarded me
    By making me the Ruler of the Queen's Navee!

CHORUS.—He thought so little, etc.

Now landsmen all, whoever you may be,
If you want to rise to the top of the tree,
If your soul isn't fettered to an office stool,
Be careful to be guided by this golden rule—
    Stick close to your desks and never go to sea,
    And you all may be Rulers of the Queen's Navee!

CHORUS.—Stick close, etc.

SIR JOSEPH. You've a remarkably fine crew, Captain Corcoran.
CAPT. It *is* a fine crew, Sir Joseph.
SIR JOSEPH (*examining* TOM TUCKER, *a very small midshipman*). A British sailor is a splendid fellow, Captain Corcoran.

CAPT. A splendid fellow indeed, Sir Joseph.

SIR JOSEPH. I hope you treat your crew kindly, Captain Corcoran.

CAPT. Indeed I hope so, Sir Joseph.

SIR JOSEPH. Never forget that they are the bulwarks of England's greatness, Captain Corcoran.

CAPT. So I have always considered them, Sir Joseph.

SIR JOSEPH. No bullying, I trust—no strong language of any kind, eh?

CAPT. Oh, never, Sir Joseph.

SIR JOSEPH. What, *never?*

CAPT. Hardly ever, Sir Joseph. They are an excellent crew, and do their work thoroughly without it.

SIR JOSEPH. Don't patronise them, sir—pray, don't patronise them.

CAPT. Certainly not, Sir Joseph.

SIR JOSEPH. That you are their captain is an accident of birth. I cannot permit these noble fellows to be patronised because an accident of birth has placed you above them and them below you.

CAPT. I am the last person to insult a British sailor, Sir Joseph.

SIR JOSEPH. You are the last person who did, Captain Corcoran. Desire that splendid seaman to step forward.

(DICK *comes forward.*)

SIR JOSEPH. No, no, the other splendid seaman.

CAPT. Ralph Rackstraw, three paces to the front—march!

SIR JOSEPH (*sternly*). If what?

CAPT. I beg your pardon—I don't think I understand you.

SIR JOSEPH. If you *please.*

CAPT. Oh, yes, of course. If you please. (RALPH *steps forward.*)

SIR JOSEPH. You're a remarkably fine fellow.

RALPH. Yes, your honour.

SIR JOSEPH. And a first-rate seaman, I'll be bound.

RALPH. There's not a smarter topman in the Navy, your honour, though I say it who shouldn't.

SIR JOSEPH. Not at all. Proper self-respect, nothing more. Can you dance a hornpipe?

RALPH. No, your honour.

SIR JOSEPH. That's a pity: all sailors should dance hornpipes. I will teach you one this evening, after dinner. Now tell me—don't be afraid—how does your captain treat you, eh?

RALPH. A better captain don't walk the deck, your honour.

ALL. Aye; Aye!

SIR JOSEPH. Good. I like to hear you speak well of your commanding officer; I daresay he don't deserve it, but still it does you credit. Can you sing?

RALPH. I can hum a little, your honour.

SIR JOSEPH. Then hum this at your leisure. (*Giving him MS. music.*) It is a song that I have composed for the use of the Royal Navy. It is designed to encourage independence of thought and action in the lower branches of the service, and to teach the principle that a British sailor is any man's equal,

excepting mine. Now, Captain Corcoran, a word with you in your cabin, on a tender and sentimental subject.

CAPT. Aye, aye, Sir Joseph. (*Crossing.*) Boatswain, in commemoration of this joyous occasion, see that extra grog is served out to the ship's company at seven bells.

BOAT. Beg pardon. If what, your honour?

CAPT. If what? I don't think I understand you.

BOAT. If you *please,* your honour.

CAPT. What!

SIR JOSEPH. The gentleman is quite right. If you *please.*

CAPT. (*stamping his foot impatiently*). If you *please!*

[*Exit.*

SIR JOSEPH.	For I hold that on the seas The expression, "if you please," A particularly gentlemanly tone implants.
COUSIN HEBE.	And so do his sisters, and his cousins, and his aunts!
ALL.	And so do his sisters, and his cousins, and his aunts!

[*Exeunt* SIR JOSEPH *and* RELATIVES.

BOAT. Ah! Sir Joseph's a true gentleman; courteous and considerate to the very humblest.

RALPH. True, Boatswain, but we are not the very humblest. Sir Joseph has explained our true position to us. As he says, a British seaman is any man's equal excepting his, and if Sir Joseph says that, is it not our duty to believe him?

ALL. Well spoke! well spoke!

DICK. You're on a wrong tack, and so is he. He means well, but he don't know. When people have to obey other people's orders, equality's out of the question.

ALL (*recoiling*). Horrible! horrible!

BOAT. Dick Deadeye, if you go for to infuriate this here ship's company too far, I won't answer for being able to hold 'em in. I'm shocked! that's what I am—shocked!

RALPH. Messmates, my mind's made up. I'll speak to the captain's daughter, and tell her, like an honest man, of the honest love I have for her.

ALL. Aye, aye!

RALPH. Is not my love as good as another's? Is not my heart as true as another's? Have I not hands and eyes and ears and limbs like another?

ALL. Aye, aye!

RALPH. True, I lack birth—

BOAT. You've a berth on board this very ship.

RALPH. Well said—I had forgotten that. Messmates—what do you say? Do you approve my determination?

ALL. We do.

DICK. *I* don't.

BOAT. What is to be done with this here hopeless chap? Let us sing him the song that Sir Joseph has kindly composed for us. Perhaps it will bring this here miserable creetur to a proper state of mind.

And we are his sisters, and his cousins, and his aunts!

GLEE—RALPH, BOATSWAIN, CARPENTER'S MATE, *and* CHORUS

A British tar is a soaring soul,
　　As free as a mountain bird,
His energetic fist should be ready to resist
　　A dictatorial word.
His nose should pant and his lip should curl,
His cheeks should flame and his brow should furl,
His bosom should heave and his heart should glow,
And his fist be ever ready for a knock-down blow.

CHORUS.—His nose should pant, etc.

His eyes should flash with an inborn fire,
　　His brow with scorn be wrung;
He never should bow down to a domineering frown,
　　Or the tang of a tyrant tongue.
His foot should stamp and his throat should growl,
His hair should twirl and his face should scowl;
His eyes should flash and his breast protrude,
And this should be his customary attitude—(*pose*).

CHORUS.—His foot should stamp, etc.

[*All dance off excepting* RALPH, *who remains, leaning pensively against bulwark.*

Enter JOSEPHINE *from cabin*

JOS. It is useless—Sir Joseph's attentions nauseate me. I know that he is a truly great and good man, for he told me so himself, but to me he seems tedious, fretful, and dictatorial. Yet his must be a mind of no common order, or he would not dare to teach my dear father to dance a hornpipe on the cabin table. (*Sees* RALPH.) Ralph Rackstraw! (*Overcome by emotion.*)

RALPH. Aye, lady—no other than poor Ralph Rackstraw!

JOS. (*aside*). How my heart beats! (*Aloud.*) And why poor, Ralph?

RALPH. I am poor in the essence of happiness, lady—rich only in never-ending unrest. In me there meet a combination of antithetical elements which are at eternal war with one another. Driven hither by objective influences—thither by subjective emotions—wafted one moment into blazing day, by mocking hope—plunged the next into the Cimmerian darkness of tangible despair, I am but a living ganglion of irreconcilable antagonisms. I hope I make myself clear, lady?

JOS. Perfectly. (*Aside.*) His simple eloquence goes to my heart. Oh, if I dared—but no, the thought is madness! (*Aloud.*) Dismiss these foolish fancies, they torture you but needlessly. Come, make one effort.

RALPH (*aside*). I will—one. (*Aloud.*) Josephine!

JOS. (*indignantly*). Sir!

RALPH. Aye, even though Jove's armoury were launched at the head of the audacious mortal whose lips, unhallowed by relationship, dared to breathe that precious word, yet would I breathe it once, and then perchance be silent evermore. Josephine, in one brief breath I will concentrate the hopes, the doubts, the anxious fears of six weary months. Josephine, I am a British sailor, and I love you!

JOS. Sir, this audacity! (*Aside.*) Oh, my heart, my beating heart! (*Aloud.*) This unwarrantable presumption on the part of a common sailor! (*Aside.*) Common! oh, the irony of the word! (*Crossing, aloud.*) Oh, sir, you forget the disparity in our ranks.

RALPH. I forget nothing, haughty lady. I love you desperately, my life is in your hand—I lay it at your feet! Give me hope, and what I lack in education and polite accomplishments, that I will endeavour to acquire. Drive me to despair, and in death alone I shall look for consolation. I am proud and cannot stoop to implore. I have spoken and I wait your word.

JOS. You shall not wait long. Your proffered love I haughtily reject. Go, sir, and learn to cast your eyes on some village maiden in your own poor rank—they should be lowered before your captain's daughter.

DUET—JOSEPHINE *and* RALPH

JOS.　　　Refrain, audacious tar,
　　　　　　Your suit from pressing,
　　　　　Remember what you are,
　　　　　　And whom addressing!
(*Aside.*)　I'd laugh my rank to scorn
　　　　　　In union holy,
　　　　　Were he more highly born
　　　　　　Or I more lowly!

RALPH.　　Proud lady, have your way,
　　　　　　Unfeeling beauty!
　　　　　You speak and I obey,
　　　　　　It is my duty!
　　　　　I am the lowliest tar
　　　　　　That sails the water,
　　　　　And you, proud maiden, are
　　　　　　My captain's daughter!
(*Aside.*)　My heart with anguish torn
　　　　　　Bows down before her,
　　　　　She laughs my love to scorn,
　　　　　　Yet I adore her!

[*Repeat refrain, ensemble, then exit* JOSEPHINE *into cabin.*

RECITATIVE—RALPH

Can I survive this overbearing
Or live a life of mad despairing,
My proffered love despised, rejected?
No, no, it's not to be expected!
　　　　　　(*Calling off.*)
Messmates, ahoy!
　　Come here! Come here!

Enter SAILORS, HEBE, *and* RELATIVES

ALL.　　　Aye, aye, my boy,
　　　　　What cheer, what cheer?
　　　　　　Now tell us, pray,
　　　　　　Without delay,
　　　　　What does she say—
　　　　　What cheer, what cheer?

And I copied all the letters in a big round hand—

RALPH (*to* COUSIN HEBE).

> The maiden treats my suit with scorn,
> Rejects my humble gift, my lady;
> She says I am ignobly born,
> And cuts my hopes adrift, my lady.

ALL.   Oh, cruel one.

DICK.   She spurns your suit? Oho! Oho!
> I told you so, I told you so.

SAILORS *and* RELATIVES.

> Shall | we / they | submit? Are | we / they | but slaves?
> Love comes alike to high and low—
> Britannia's sailors rule the waves,
> And shall they stoop to insult? No!

DICK.   You must submit, you are but slaves;
> A lady she! Oho! Oho!
> You lowly toilers of the waves,
> She spurns you all—I told you so!

RALPH.   My friends, my leave of life I'm taking,
> For oh, my heart, my heart is breaking.
> When I am gone, oh, prithee tell
> The maid that, as I died, I loved her well!

ALL (*turning away, weeping*).

> Of life, alas! his leave he's taking,
> For ah! his faithful heart is breaking;
> When he is gone we'll surely tell
> The maid that, as he died, he loved her well.

[*During Chorus* BOATSWAIN *has loaded pistol, which he hands to* RALPH.

RALPH.   Be warned, my messmates all
> Who love in rank above you—
> For Josephine I fall!

[*Puts pistol to his head. All the sailors stop their ears.*

Enter JOSEPHINE *on deck*

JOS.   Ah! stay your hand! I love you!
ALL.   Ah! stay your hand—she loves you!
RALPH (*incredulously*). Loves me?
JOS.   Loves you!
ALL.   Yes, yes—ah, yes,—she loves you!

ENSEMBLE
SAILORS *and* RELATIVES *and* JOSEPHINE

Oh joy, oh rapture unforeseen,
For now the sky is all serene;
The god of day—the orb of love—
Has hung his ensign high above,
    The sky is all ablaze.

With wooing words and loving song,
We'll chase the lagging hours along,

> And if | I find / we find | the maiden coy,
> I'll / We'll | murmur forth decorous joy
>   In dreamy roundelays!

DICK DEADEYE
He thinks he's won his Josephine,
But though the sky is now serene,
A frowning thunderbolt above
May end their ill-assorted love
    Which now is all ablaze.
Our captain, ere the day is gone,
Will be extremely down upon
The wicked men who art employ
To make his Josephine less coy
    In many various ways.

[*Exit* DICK.

JOS.   This very night,
HEBE.   With bated breath
RALPH.   And muffled oar—
JOS.   Without a light,
HEBE.   As still as death,
RALPH.   We'll steal ashore
JOS.   A clergyman
RALPH.   Shall make us one
BOAT.   At half-past ten,
JOS.   And then we can
RALPH.   Return, for none
BOAT.   Can part them then!
ALL.   This very night, etc.

(DICK *appears at hatchway.*)

DICK.   Forbear, nor carry out the scheme you've planned;
> She is a lady—you a foremast hand!
> Remember, she's your gallant captain's daughter,
> And you the meanest slave that crawls the water!

ALL.   Back, vermin, back,
>   Nor mock us!
> Back, vermin, back,
>   You shock us!

[*Exit* DICK.

Let's give three cheers for the sailor's bride
Who casts all thought of rank aside—
Who gives up home and fortune too
For the honest love of a sailor true!
    For a British tar is a soaring soul
        As free as a mountain bird!
    His energetic fist should be ready to resist
        A dictatorial word!
His foot should stamp and his throat should growl,
His hair should twirl and his face should scowl,
His eyes should flash and his breast protrude,
And this should be his customary attitude—(*pose*).

GENERAL DANCE

END OF ACT I

ACT II

Same Scene. Night. Awning removed. Moonlight. CAPTAIN *discovered singing on poop-deck, and accompanying himself on a mandolin.* LITTLE BUTTERCUP *seated on quarter-deck, gazing sentimentally at him.*

SONG—CAPTAIN

Fair moon, to thee I sing,
 Bright regent of the heavens,
Say, why is everything
 Either at sixes or at sevens?
I have lived hitherto
 Free from breath of slander,
Beloved by all my crew—
 A really popular commander.
But now my kindly crew rebel,
 My daughter to a tar is partial,
Sir Joseph storms, and, sad to tell,
 He threatens a court martial!
 Fair moon, to thee I sing,
  Bright regent of the heavens,
 Say, why is everything
  Either at sixes or at sevens?

BUT. How sweetly he carols forth his melody to the unconscious moon! Of whom is he thinking? Of some high-born beauty! It may be! Who is poor Little Buttercup that she should expect his glance to fall on one so lowly! And yet if he knew—if he only knew!

CAPT. (*coming down*). Ah! Little Buttercup, still on board? That is not quite right, little one. It would have been more respectable to have gone on shore at dusk.

BUT. True, dear Captain—but the recollection of your sad pale face seemed to chain me to the ship. I would fain see you smile before I go.

CAPT. Ah! Little Buttercup, I fear it will be long before I recover my accustomed cheerfulness, for misfortunes crowd upon me, and all my old friends seem to have turned against me!

BUT. Oh no—do not say "all," dear Captain. That were unjust to one, at least.

CAPT. True, for you are staunch to me. (*Aside.*) If ever I gave my heart again, methinks it would be to such a one as this! (*Aloud.*) I am touched to the heart by your innocent regard for me, and were we differently situated, I think I could have returned it. But as it is, I fear I can never be more to you than a friend.

BUT. I understand! You hold aloof from me because you are rich and lofty—and I poor and lowly. But take care! The poor bumboat woman has gipsy blood in her veins, and she can read destinies.

CAPT. Destinies?

BUT. There is a change in store for you!

CAPT. A change?

BUT. Aye—be prepared!

DUET—BUTTERCUP *and* CAPTAIN

BUT. Things are seldom what they seem,
  Skim milk masquerades as cream;
  Highlows pass as patent leathers;
  Jackdaws strut in peacock's feathers.

CAPT. (*puzzled*). Very true,
   So they do.

BUT. Black sheep dwell in every fold;
  All that glitters is not gold;
  Storks turn out to be but logs;
  Bulls are but inflated frogs.

CAPT. (*puzzled*). So they be,
   Frequentlee.

BUT. Drops the wind and stops the mill;
  Turbot is ambitious brill;
  Gild the farthing if you will,
  Yet it is a farthing still.

CAPT. (*puzzled*). Yes, I know.
   That is so.
  Though to catch your drift I'm striving,
   It is shady—it is shady;
  I don't see at what you're driving,
   Mystic lady—mystic lady,

(*Aside.*) Stern conviction's o'er me stealing,
  That the mystic lady's dealing
  In oracular revealing.

BUT. (*aside*). Stern conviction's o'er him stealing,
  That the mystic lady's dealing
  In oracular revealing.

BOTH. Yes, I know—
   That is so!

CAPT. Though I'm anything but clever,
  I could talk like that for ever:
  Once a cat was killed by care;
  Only brave deserve the fair.

BUT. Very true,
   So they do.

CAPT. Wink is often good as nod;
  Spoils the child who spares the rod;
  Thirsty lambs run foxy dangers;
  Dogs are found in many mangers.

BUT. Frequentlee,
   I agree.

CAPT. Paw of cat the chestnut snatches;
  Worn-out garments show new patches;
  Only count the chick that hatches;
  Men are grown-up catchy-catchies.

BUT. Yes, I know,
   That is so.

(*Aside.*) Though to catch my drift he's striving,
   I'll dissemble—I'll dissemble;
  When he sees at what I'm driving,
   Let him tremble—let him tremble!

ENSEMBLE

Though a mystic tone $\left\{\begin{array}{l} I \\ you \end{array}\right.$ borrow,
You will $\left.\begin{array}{l}\\\\\end{array}\right\}$
I shall $\left.\begin{array}{l}\\\end{array}\right.$ learn the truth with sorrow,
Here to-day and gone to-morrow;
    Yes, I know—
That is so!

[*At the end exit* LITTLE BUTTERCUP *melodramatically.*

CAPT. Incomprehensible as her utterances are, I nevertheless feel that they are dictated by a sincere regard for me. But to what new misery is she referring? Time alone can tell!

Enter SIR JOSEPH

SIR JOSEPH. Captain Corcoran, I am much disappointed with your daughter. In fact, I don't think she will do.

CAPT. She won't do, Sir Joseph!

SIR JOSEPH. I'm afraid not. The fact is, that although I have urged my suit with as much eloquence as is consistent with an official utterance, I have done so hitherto without success. How do you account for this?

CAPT. Really, Sir Joseph, I hardly know. Josephine is of course sensible of your condescension.

SIR JOSEPH. She naturally would be.

CAPT. But perhaps your exalted rank dazzles her.

SIR JOSEPH. You think it does?

CAPT. I can hardly say; but she is a modest girl, and her social position is far below your own. It may be that she feels she is not worthy of you.

SIR JOSEPH. That is really a very sensible suggestion, and displays more knowledge of human nature than I had given you credit for.

CAPT. See, she comes. If your lordship would kindly reason with her and assure her officially that it is a standing rule at the Admiralty that love levels all ranks, her respect for an official utterance might induce her to look upon your offer in its proper light.

SIR JOSEPH. It is not unlikely. I will adopt your suggestion. But soft, she is here. Let us withdraw, and watch our opportunity.

Enter JOSEPHINE *from cabin.* FIRST LORD *and*
CAPTAIN *retire*

SCENA—JOSEPHINE

The hours creep on apace,
  My guilty heart is quaking!
Oh, that I might retrace
  The step that I am taking!
Its folly it were easy to be showing,
What I am giving up and whither going.
On the one hand, papa's luxurious home,
  Hung with ancestral armour and old brasses,
Carved oak and tapestry from distant Rome,

Rare "blue and white" Venetian finger-glasses,
Rich oriental rugs, luxurious sofa pillows,
And everything that isn't old, from Gillow's.
And on the other, a dark and dingy room,
  In some back street with stuffy children crying,
Where organs yell, and clacking housewives fume,
  And clothes are hanging out all day a-drying.
With one cracked looking-glass to see your face in,
And dinner served up in a pudding basin!

A simple sailor, lowly born,
  Unlettered and unknown,
Who toils for bread from early morn
  Till half the night has flown!
No golden rank can he impart—
  No wealth of house or land—
No fortune save his trusty heart
  And honest brown right hand!
And yet he is so wondrous fair
That love for one so passing rare,
So peerless in his manly beauty,
Were little else than solemn duty!
Oh, god of love, and god of reason, say,
Which of you twain shall my poor heart obey!

SIR JOSEPH *and* CAPTAIN *enter*

SIR JOSEPH. Madam, it has been represented to me that you are appalled by my exalted rank. I desire to convey to you officially my assurance, that if your hesitation is attributable to that circumstance, it is uncalled for.

JOS. Oh! then your lordship is of opinion that married happiness is *not* inconsistent with discrepancy in rank?

SIR JOSEPH. I am officially of that opinion.

JOS. That the high and the lowly may be truly happy together, provided that they truly love one another?

SIR JOSEPH. Madam, I desire to convey to you officially my opinion that love is a platform upon which all ranks meet.

JOS. I thank you, Sir Joseph. I *did* hesitate, but I will hesitate no longer. (*Aside.*) He little thinks how eloquently he has pleaded his rival's cause!

TRIO
FIRST LORD, CAPTAIN, *and* JOSEPHINE

CAPT.
    Never mind the why and wherefore,
    Love can level ranks, and therefore,
    Though his lordship's station's mighty,
      Though stupendous be his brain,
    Though your tastes are mean and flighty
      And your fortune poor and plain,

CAPT. *and*
SIR JOSEPH.
    Ring the merry bells on board-ship,
      Rend the air with warbling wild,

For the union of $\left\{\begin{array}{l} his \\ my \end{array}\right.$ lordship
    With a humble captain's child!

24

I thought so little, they rewarded me / By making me the Ruler of the Queen's Navee!

CAPT.   For a humble captain's daughter—
JOS.   For a gallant captain's daughter—
SIR JOSEPH.   And a lord who rules the water—
JOS. (*aside*).   And a *tar* who ploughs the water!
ALL.   Let the air with joy be laden,
       Rend with songs the air above,
       For the union of a maiden
       With the man who owns her love!

SIR JOSEPH.   Never mind the why and wherefore,
       Love can level ranks, and therefore,
       Though your nautical relation (*alluding to*
                         CAPT.)
       In my set could scarcely pass—
       Though you occupy a station
       In the lower middle class—
CAPT. *and*   Ring the merry bells on board-ship,
SIR JOSEPH.   Rend the air with warbling wild,
       For the union of | my / his | lordship
       With a humble captain's child!
CAPT.   For a humble captain's daughter—
JOS.   For a gallant captain's daughter—
SIR JOSEPH.   And a lord who rules the water—
JOS. (*aside*).   And a *tar* who ploughs the water!
ALL.   Let the air with joy be laden,
       Rend with songs the air above,
       For the union of a maiden
       With the man who owns her love!

JOS.   Never mind the why and wherefore,
       Love can level ranks, and therefore
       I admit the jurisdiction;
       Ably have you played your part;
       You have carried firm conviction
       To my hesitating heart.
CAPT. *and*   Ring the merry bells on board-ship,
SIR JOSEPH.   Rend the air with warbling wild,
       For the union of | my / his | lordship
       With a humble captain's child!
CAPT.   For a humble captain's daughter—
JOS.   For a gallant captain's daughter—
SIR JOSEPH.   And a lord who rules the water—
JOS. (*aside*).   And a *tar* who ploughs the water!
(*Aloud.*)   Let the air with joy be laden.
CAPT. *and* SIR JOSEPH. Ring the merry bells on board-ship—
JOS.   For the union of a maiden—
CAPT. *and* SIR JOSEPH. For her union with his lordship.
ALL.   Rend with songs the air above
       For the man who owns her love!
                        [*Exit* JOS.

CAPT. Sir Joseph, I cannot express to you my delight at the happy result of your eloquence. Your argument was unanswerable.

SIR JOSEPH. Captain Corcoran, it is one of the happiest characteristics of this glorious country that official utterances are invariably regarded as unanswerable.

                        [*Exit* SIR JOSEPH.

CAPT. At last my fond hopes are to be crowned. My only daughter is to be the bride of a Cabinet Minister. The prospect is Elysian. (*During this speech* DICK DEADEYE *has entered.*)

DICK. Captain.

CAPT. Deadeye! You here? Don't! (*Recoiling from him.*)

DICK. Ah, don't shrink from me, Captain. I'm unpleasant to look at, and my name's agin me, but I ain't as bad as I seem.

CAPT. What would you with me?

DICK (*mysteriously*). I'm come to give you warning.

CAPT. Indeed! do you propose to leave the Navy then?

DICK. No, no, you misunderstand me; listen!

DUET
CAPTAIN *and* DICK DEADEYE

DICK.   Kind Captain, I've important information,
       Sing hey, the kind commander that you are,
       About a certain intimate relation,
       Sing hey, the merry maiden and the tar.
BOTH.   The merry maiden and the tar.

CAPT.   Good fellow, in conundrums you are speaking,
       Sing hey, the mystic sailor that you are;
       The answer to them vainly I am seeking;
       Sing hey, the merry maiden and the tar.
BOTH.   The merry maiden and the tar.

DICK.   Kind Captain, your young lady is a-sighing,
       Sing hey, the simple captain that you are,
       This very night with Rackstraw to be flying;
       Sing hey, the merry maiden and the tar.
BOTH.   The merry maiden and the tar.

CAPT.   Good fellow, you have given timely warning,
       Sing hey, the thoughtful sailor that you are,
       I'll talk to Master Rackstraw in the morning:
       Sing hey, the cat-o'-nine-tails and the tar.

                    (*Producing a "cat".*)

BOTH.   The merry cat-o'-nine-tails and the tar!

CAPT. Dick Deadeye—I thank you for your warning—I will at once take means to arrest their flight. This boat cloak will afford me ample disguise—So! (*Envelops himself in a mysterious cloak, holding it before his face.*)

DICK. Ha, ha! They are foiled—foiled—foiled!

Enter Crew on tiptoe, with RALPH *and* BOATSWAIN *meeting* JOSEPHINE, *who enters from cabin on tiptoe, with bundle of necessaries, and accompanied by* LITTLE BUTTERCUP.

ENSEMBLE

Carefully on tiptoe stealing,
    Breathing gently as we may,
Every step with caution feeling,
    We will softly steal away.

(CAPTAIN *stamps.*)–*Chord.*

ALL (*much alarmed*). Goodness me–
        Why, what was that?
DICK.   Silent be,
        It was the cat!
ALL (*reassured*). It was–it was the cat!
CAPT. (*producing cat-o'-nine-tails*). They're right, it was the cat!

ALL.   Pull ashore, in fashion steady,
      Hymen will defray the fare,
    For a clergyman is ready
      To unite the happy pair!

(*Stamp as before, and Chord.*)

ALL.   Goodness me,
          Why, what was that?
DICK.   Silent be,
          Again the cat!
ALL.   It was again that cat!
CAPT. (*aside*).   They're right, it was the cat!
CAPT. (*throwing off cloak*). Hold! (*All start.*)
        Pretty daughter of mine,
        I insist upon knowing
        Where you may be going
        With these sons of the brine,
        For my excellent crew,
        Though foes they could thump any,
        Are scarcely fit company,
        My daughter, for you.
CREW.   Now, hark at that, do!
        Though foes we could thump any,
        We are scarcely fit company
        For a lady like you!

RALPH.   Proud officer, that haughty lip uncurl!
    Vain man, suppress that supercilious sneer,
For I have dared to love your matchless girl,
    A fact well known to all my messmates here!

CAPT.   Oh, horror!

RALPH *and* JOS. $\left\{\begin{array}{l}\text{I,}\\\text{He,}\end{array}\right\}$ humble, poor, and lowly born,
    The meanest in the port division–
    The butt of epauletted scorn–
    The mark of quarter-deck derision–
    $\left.\begin{array}{l}\text{Have}\\\text{Has}\end{array}\right\}$ dared to raise $\left\{\begin{array}{l}\text{my}\\\text{his}\end{array}\right\}$ wormy eyes

    Above the dust to which you'd mould $\left\{\begin{array}{l}\text{me}\\\text{him}\end{array}\right.$

In manhood's glorious pride to rise,
$\left.\begin{array}{l}\text{I am}\\\text{He is}\end{array}\right\}$ an Englishman–behold $\left\{\begin{array}{l}\text{me!}\\\text{him!}\end{array}\right.$

ALL.   He is an Englishman!
BOAT.   He is an Englishman!
      For he himself has said it,
      And it's greatly to his credit,
      That he is an Englishman!
ALL.   That he is an Englishman!
BOAT.   For he might have been a Roosian,
    A French, or Turk, or Proosian,
    Or perhaps Itali-an!
ALL.   Or perhaps Itali-an!
BOAT.   But in spite of all temptations
    To belong to other nations,
      He remains an Englishman!
ALL.   For in spite of all temptations, etc.

CAPT. (*trying to repress his anger*).
      In uttering a reprobation
        To any British tar,
    I try to speak with moderation,
      But you have gone too far.
    I'm very sorry to disparage
      A humble foremast lad,
    But to seek your captain's child in marriage,
      Why damme, it's too bad!

[*During this,* COUSIN HEBE *and* FEMALE RELATIVES *have entered.*

ALL (*shocked*).   Oh!
CAPT.   Yes, damme, it's too bad!
ALL.   Oh!
CAPT. *and* DICK DEADEYE. Yes, damme, it's too bad!

[*During this,* SIR JOSEPH *has appeared on poop-deck. He is horrified at the bad language.*

HEBE.   Did you hear him–did you hear him?
      Oh, the monster overbearing!
    Don't go near him–don't go near him–
      He is swearing–he is swearing!
SIR JOSEPH.   My pain and my distress,
      I find it is not easy to express;
      My amazement–my surprise–
    You may learn from the expression of my
      eyes!
CAPT.   My lord–one word–the facts are not before
      you
    The word was injudicious, I allow–
    But hear my explanation, I implore you,
      And you will be indignant too, I vow!
SIR JOSEPH.   I will hear of no defence,
      Attempt none if you're sensible.
    That word of evil sense

Is wholly indefensible.
Go, ribald, get you hence
To your cabin with celerity.
This is the consequence
Of ill-advised asperity!

[*Exit* CAPTAIN, *disgraced, followed by* JOSEPHINE.

ALL.   This is the consequence,
Of ill-advised asperity!

SIR JOSEPH.   For I'll teach you all, ere long,
To refrain from language strong
For I haven't any sympathy for ill-bred
taunts!

HEBE.   No more have his sisters, nor his cousins, nor
his aunts.

ALL.   For he is an Englishman, etc.

SIR JOSEPH. Now, tell me, my fine fellow—for you *are* a fine
fellow—

RALPH. Yes, your honour.

SIR JOSEPH. How came your captain so far to forget himself? I am quite sure you had given him no cause for
annoyance.

RALPH. Please your honour, it was thus-wise. You see I'm
only a topman—a mere foremast hand—

SIR JOSEPH. Don't be ashamed of that. Your position as a
topman is a very exalted one.

RALPH. Well, your honour, love burns as brightly in the
fo'c'sle as it does on the quarter-deck, and Josephine is the
fairest bud that ever blossomed upon the tree of a poor fellow's wildest hopes.

Enter JOSEPHINE; *she rushes to* RALPH'S *arms*

JOS. Darling! (SIR JOSEPH *horrified.*)

RALPH. She is the figurehead of my ship of life—the bright
beacon that guides me into my port of happiness—the rarest,
the purest gem that ever sparkled on a poor but worthy
fellow's trusting brow!

ALL. Very pretty, very pretty!

SIR JOSEPH. Insolent sailor, you shall repent this outrage.
Seize him!

(*Two Marines seize him and handcuff him.*)

JOS. Oh, Sir Joseph, spare him, for I love him tenderly.

SIR JOSEPH. Pray, don't. I will teach this presumptuous
mariner to discipline his affections. Have you such a thing as
a dungeon on board?

ALL. We have!

DICK. They have!

SIR JOSEPH. Then load him with chains and take him there
at once!

OCTETTE

RALPH.   Farewell, my own,
Light of my life, farewell!
For crime unknown
I go to a dungeon cell.

JOS.   I will atone.
In the meantime farewell!

And all alone
Rejoice in your dungeon cell!

SIR JOSEPH.   A bone, a bone
I'll pick with this sailor fell;
Let him be shown
At once to his dungeon cell.

BOATSWAIN, DICK DEADEYE, *and* COUSIN HEBE

He'll hear no tone
Of the maiden he loves so well!
No telephone
Communicates with his cell!

BUT. (*mysteriously*). But when is known
The secret I have to tell,
Wide will be thrown
The door of his dungeon cell.

ALL.   For crime unknown
He goes to a dungeon cell!

[RALPH *is led off in custody.*

SIR JOSEPH.   My pain and my distress
Again it is not easy to express.
My amazement, my surprise,
Again you may discover from my eyes.

ALL.   How terrible the aspect of his eyes!

BUT.   Hold! Ere upon your loss
You lay much stress,
A long-concealèd crime
I would confess.

SONG—BUTTERCUP

A many years ago,
When I was young and charming,
As some of you may know,
I practised baby-farming.

ALL.   Now this is most alarming!
When she was young and charming,
She practised baby-farming,
A many years ago.

BUT.   Two tender babes I nussed:
One was of low condition,
The other, upper crust,
A regular patrician.

ALL (*explaining to each other*).
Now, this is the position:
One was of low condition,
The other a patrician,
A many years ago.

BUT.   Oh, bitter is my cup!
However could I do it?
I mixed those children up,
And not a creature knew it!

ALL.   However could you do it?
Some day, no doubt, you'll rue it,

Things are seldom what they seem, . . .

Although no creature knew it,
So many years ago.

BUT. In time each little waif
Forsook his foster-mother,
The well-born babe was Ralph—
Your captain was the other!!!

ALL. They left their foster-mother,
The one was Ralph, our brother,
Our captain was the other,
A many years ago.

SIR JOSEPH. Then I am to understand that Captain Corcoran and Ralph were exchanged in childhood's happy hour—that Ralph is really the Captain, and the Captain is Ralph?

BUT. That is the idea I intended to convey, officially!

SIR JOSEPH. And very well you have conveyed it.

BUT. Aye! aye! yer 'onour.

SIR JOSEPH. Dear me! Let them appear before me, at once!

RALPH *enters as* CAPTAIN; CAPTAIN *as a common sailor.* JOSEPHINE *rushes to his arms*

JOS. My father—a common sailor!

CAPT. It is hard, is it not, my dear?

SIR JOSEPH. This is a very singular occurrence; I congratulate you both. (*To* RALPH.) Desire that remarkably fine seaman to step forward.

RALPH. Corcoran. Three paces to the front—march!

CAPT. If what?

RALPH. If what? I don't think I understand you.

CAPT. If you please.

SIR JOSEPH. The gentleman is quite right. If you *please.*

RALPH. Oh! If you *please.* (CAPTAIN *steps forward.*)

SIR JOSEPH (*to* CAPTAIN). You are an extremely fine fellow.

CAPT. Yes, your honour.

SIR JOSEPH. So it seems that you were Ralph, and Ralph was you.

CAPT. So it seems, your honour.

SIR JOSEPH. Well, I need not tell you that after this change in your condition, a marriage with your daughter will be out of the question.

CAPT. Don't say that, your honour—love levels all ranks.

SIR JOSEPH. It does to a considerable extent, but it does not level them as much as that. (*Handing* JOSEPHINE *to* RALPH.) Here—take her, sir, and mind you treat her kindly.

RALPH *and* JOS. Oh bliss, oh rapture!

CAPT. *and* BUT. Oh rapture, oh bliss!

SIR JOSEPH.   Sad my lot and sorry,
What shall I do? I cannot live alone!

HEBE. Fear nothing—while I live I'll not desert you.
I'll soothe and comfort your declining days.

SIR JOSEPH.   No, don't do that.

HEBE.   Yes, but indeed I'd rather—

SIR JOSEPH (*resigned*). To-morrow morn our vows shall all
be plighted,
Three loving pairs on the same day united!

QUARTETTE
JOSEPHINE, HEBE, RALPH, *and* DEADEYE

Oh joy, oh rapture unforeseen,
The clouded sky is now serene,
The god of day—the orb of love,
Has hung his ensign high above,
The sky is all ablaze.

With wooing words and loving song,
We'll chase the lagging hours along,
And if │ he finds │ the maiden coy,
       │ I find │
We'll murmur forth decorous joy,
In dreamy roundelay.

CAPT. For he's the Captain of the *Pinafore.*

ALL. And a right good captain too!

CAPT.   And though before my fall
I was captain of you all,
I'm a member of the crew.

ALL.   Although before his fall, etc.

CAPT. I shall marry with a wife,
In my humble rank of life! (*turning to* BUT.)
And you, my own, are she—
I must wander to and fro;
But wherever I may go,
I shall never be untrue to thee!

ALL.   What, never?

CAPT.   No, never!

ALL.   What, *never?*

CAPT.   Hardly ever!

ALL.   Hardly ever be untrue to thee.
Then give three cheers, and one cheer more
For the former Captain of the *Pinafore.*

BUT. For he loves Little Buttercup, dear Little
Buttercup,
Though I could never tell why;
But still he loves Buttercup, poor Little
Buttercup,
Sweet Little Buttercup, aye!

ALL.   For he loves, etc.

SIR JOSEPH. I'm the monarch of the sea,
And when I've married thee (*to* HEBE),
I'll be true to the devotion that my love
implants,

HEBE. Then good-bye to his sisters, and his cousins,
and his aunts,
Especially his cousins,
Whom he reckons up by dozens,
His sisters, and his cousins, and his aunts!

ALL. For he is an Englishman,
And he himself hath said it,
And it's greatly to his credit
That he is an Englishman!

CURTAIN

30

THE PIRATES of PENZANCE

THE PIRATES of PENZANCE
OR, THE SLAVE of DUTY

DRAMATIS PERSONÆ

MAJOR-GENERAL STANLEY

THE PIRATE KING

SAMUEL (*his Lieutenant*)

FREDERIC (*the Pirate Apprentice*)

SERGEANT OF POLICE

MABEL

EDITH

KATE   } (*General Stanley's Daughters*)

ISABEL

RUTH (*a Pirate Maid of all Work*)

*Chorus of Pirates, Police, and General Stanley's
Daughters*

A C T I

A ROCKY SEA-SHORE ON THE COAST OF CORNWALL

A C T II

A RUINED CHAPEL BY MOONLIGHT

First produced at the Opéra Comique on April 3, 1880

THE PIRATES of PENZANCE
OR, THE SLAVE of DUTY

ACT I

SCENE.—*A rocky sea-shore on the coast of Cornwall. In the distance is a calm sea, on which a schooner is lying at anchor. As the curtain rises groups of pirates are discovered—some drinking, some playing cards.* SAMUEL, *the Pirate Lieutenant, is going from one group to another, filling the cups from a flask.* FREDERIC *is seated in a despondent attitude at the back of the scene.*

OPENING CHORUS

> Pour, oh, pour the pirate sherry;
>   Fill, oh, fill the pirate glass;
> And, to make us more than merry,
>   Let the pirate bumper pass.

SAM.
> For to-day our pirate 'prentice
>   Rises from indenture freed;
> Strong his arm and keen his scent is,
>   He's a pirate now indeed!

ALL.
> Here's good luck to Frederic's ventures!
> Frederic's out of his indentures.

SAM.
> Two-and-twenty now he's rising,
>   And alone he's fit to fly,
> Which we're bent on signalizing
>   With unusual revelry.

ALL.
> Here's good luck to Frederic's ventures!
> Frederic's out of his indentures,
> Pour, oh, pour the pirate sherry, etc.

FREDERIC *rises and comes forward with* PIRATE KING, *who enters*

KING. Yes, Frederic, from to-day you rank as a full-blown member of our band.

ALL. Hurrah.

FRED. My friends, I thank you all, from my heart, for your kindly wishes. Would that I could repay them as they deserve!

KING. What do you mean?

FRED. To-day I am out of my indentures, and to-day I leave you for ever.

KING. But this is quite unaccountable; a keener hand at scuttling a Cunarder or cutting out a P. & O. never shipped a handspike.

FRED. Yes, I have done my best for you. And why? It was my duty under my indentures, and I am the slave of duty. As a child I was regularly apprenticed to your band. It was through an error—no matter, the mistake was ours, not yours, and I was in honour bound by it.

SAM. An error? What error?

RUTH *enters*

FRED. I may not tell you; it would reflect upon my well-loved Ruth.

RUTH. Nay, dear master, my mind has long been gnawed by the cankering tooth of mystery. Better have it out at once.

SONG—RUTH

When Frederic was a little lad he proved so brave and
    daring,
His father thought he'd 'prentice him to some career sea-
    faring.
I was, alas! his nurserymaid, and so it fell to *my* lot
To take and bind the promising boy apprentice to a
    pilot—
A life not bad for a hardy lad, though surely not a high
    lot,
Though I'm a nurse, you might do worse than make your boy
    a pilot.

I was a stupid nurserymaid, on breakers always steering,
And I did not catch the word aright, through being hard of
    hearing;
Mistaking my instructions, which within my brain did
    gyrate,
I took and bound this promising boy apprentice to a
    pirate.
A sad mistake it was to make and doom him to a vile lot.
I bound him to a pirate—you—instead of to a pilot.

I soon found out, beyond all doubt, the scope of this
    disaster,

35

But I hadn't the face to return to my place, and break it to
my master.
A nurserymaid is not afraid of what you people *call*
work,
So I made up my mind to go as a kind of piratical maid-of-
all-work.
And that is how you find me now, a member of your shy
lot,
Which you wouldn't have found, had he been bound apprentice to a pilot.

RUTH. Oh, pardon! Frederic, pardon! (*Kneels.*)
FRED. Rise, sweet one, I have long pardoned you.
RUTH (*rises*). The two words were so much alike!
FRED. They were. They still are, though years have rolled
over their heads. But this afternoon my obligation ceases.
Individually, I love you all with affection unspeakable, but,
collectively, I look upon you with a disgust that amounts to
absolute detestation. Oh! pity me, my beloved friends, for
such is my sense of duty that, once out of my indentures, I
shall feel myself bound to devote myself heart and soul to
your extermination!
ALL. Poor lad—poor lad! (*All weep.*)
KING. Well, Frederic, if you conscientiously feel that it is
your duty to destroy us, we cannot blame you for acting on
that conviction. Always act in accordance with the dictates of
your conscience, my boy, and chance the consequences.
SAM. Besides, we can offer you but little temptation to
remain with us. We don't seem to make piracy pay. I'm sure I
don't know why, but we don't.
FRED. *I* know why, but, alas! I mustn't tell you; it
wouldn't be right.
KING. Why not, my boy? It's only half-past eleven, and
you are one of us until the clock strikes twelve.
SAM. True, and until then you are bound to protect our
interests.
ALL. Hear, hear!
FRED. Well, then, it is my duty, as a pirate, to tell you that
you are too tender-hearted. For instance, you make a point of
never attacking a weaker party than yourselves, and when you
attack a stronger party you invariably get thrashed.
KING. There is some truth in that.
FRED. Then, again, you make a point of never molesting an
orphan!
SAM. Of course: we are orphans ourselves, and know what
it is.
FRED. Yes, but it has got about, and what is the consequence? Every one we capture says he's an orphan. The last
three ships we took proved to be manned entirely by orphans,
and so we had to let them go. One would think that Great
Britain's mercantile navy was recruited solely from her orphan
asylums—which we know is not the case.
SAM. But, hang it all! you wouldn't have us absolutely
merciless?
FRED. There's my difficulty; until twelve o'clock I would,

after twelve I wouldn't. Was ever a man placed in so delicate a
situation!
RUTH. And Ruth, your own Ruth, whom you love so well,
and who has won her middle-aged way into your boyish
heart, what is to become of *her?*
KING. Oh, he will take you with him.
FRED. Well, Ruth, I feel some little difficulty about you. It
is true that I admire you very much, but I have been con-
stantly at sea since I was eight years old, and yours is the only
woman's face I have seen during that time. I think it is a
sweet face.
RUTH. It is—oh, it is!
FRED. I say I *think* it is; that is my impression. But as I
have never had an opportunity of comparing you with other
women, it is just possible I may be mistaken.
KING. True.
FRED. What a terrible thing it would be if I were to marry
this innocent person, and then find out that she is, on the
whole, plain!
KING. Oh, Ruth is very well, very well indeed.
SAM. Yes, there are the remains of a fine woman about
Ruth.
FRED. Do you really think so?
SAM. I do.
FRED. Then I will not be so selfish as to take her from you.
In justice to her, and in consideration for you, I will leave her
behind. (*Hands* RUTH *to* KING.)
KING. No, Frederic, this must not be. We are rough men
who lead a rough life, but we are not so utterly heartless as to
deprive thee of thy love. I think I am right in saying that
there is not one here who would rob thee of this inestimable
treasure for all the world holds dear.
ALL (*loudly*). Not one!
KING. No, I thought there wasn't. Keep thy love, Frederic,
keep thy love. (*Hands her back to* FREDERIC.)
FRED. You're very good, I'm sure. [*Exit* RUTH.
KING. Well, it's the top of the tide, and we must be off.
Farewell, Frederic. When your process of extermination be-
gins, let our deaths be as swift and painless as you can conve-
niently make them.
FRED. I will! By the love I have for you, I swear it! Would
that you could render this extermination unnecessary by ac-
companying me back to civilization!
KING. No, Frederic, it cannot be. I don't think much of
our profession, but, contrasted with respectability, it is com-
paratively honest. No, Frederic, I shall live and die a Pirate
King.

SONG—PIRATE KING

Oh better far to live and die
Under the brave black flag I fly,
Than play a sanctimonious part,
With a pirate head and a pirate heart.
Away to the cheating world go you,
Where pirates all are well-to-do;

I took and bound this promising boy apprentice to a pirate.

But I'll be true to the song I sing,
And live and die a Pirate King.
For I am a Pirate King.

ALL. You are!
Hurrah for our Pirate King!

KING. And it is, it is a glorious thing
To be a Pirate King.

ALL. Hurrah!
Hurrah for our Pirate King!

KING. When I sally forth to seek my prey
I help myself in a royal way:
I sink a few more ships, it's true,
Than a well-bred monarch ought to do;
But many a king on a first-class throne,
If he wants to call his crown his own,
Must manage somehow to get through
More dirty work than ever *I* do,
Though I am a Pirate King.

ALL. You are!
Hurrah for our Pirate King!

KING. And it is, it is a glorious thing
To be a Pirate King!

ALL. It is!
Hurrah for our Pirate King!

[*Exeunt all except* FREDERIC.

Enter RUTH

RUTH. Oh, take me with you! I cannot live if I am left behind.

FRED. Ruth, I will be quite candid with you. You are very dear to me, as you know, but I must be circumspect. You see, you are considerably older than I. A lad of twenty-one usually looks for a wife of seventeen.

RUTH. A wife of seventeen! You will find me a wife of a thousand!

FRED. No, but I shall find you a wife of forty-seven, and that is quite enough. Ruth, tell me candidly, and without reserve: compared with other women—how are *you?*

RUTH. I will answer you truthfully, master—I have a slight cold, but otherwise I am quite well.

FRED. I am sorry for your cold, but I was referring rather to your personal appearance. Compared with other women, are you beautiful?

RUTH (*bashfully*). I have been told so, dear master.

FRED. Ah, but lately?

RUTH. Oh, no, years and years ago.

FRED. What do you think of yourself?

RUTH. It is a delicate question to answer, but I think I am a fine woman.

FRED. That is your candid opinion?

RUTH. Yes, I should be deceiving you if I told you otherwise.

FRED. Thank you, Ruth, I believe you, for I am sure you would not practise on my inexperience; I wish to do the right

thing, and if—I say *if*—you are really a fine woman, your age shall be no obstacle to our union! (*Chorus of Girls heard in the distance.*) Hark! Surely I hear voices! Who has ventured to approach our all but inaccessible lair? Can it be Custom House? No, it does not sound like Custom House.

RUTH (*aside*). Confusion! it is the voices of young girls! If he should see them I am lost.

FRED. (*looking off*). By all that's marvellous, a bevy of beautiful maidens!

RUTH (*aside*). Lost! lost! lost!

FRED. How lovely! how surpassingly lovely is the plainest of them! What grace—what delicacy—what refinement! And Ruth—Ruth told me she was beautiful!

RECITATIVE—FRED. *and* RUTH

FRED. Oh, false one, you have deceived me!
RUTH. I have deceived you?
FRED. Yes, deceived me!

(*Denouncing her.*)

DUET—FRED. *and* RUTH

FRED. You told me you were fair as gold!
RUTH (*wildly*). And, master, am I not so?
FRED. And now I see you're plain and old.
RUTH. I am sure I am not a jot so.
FRED. Upon my innocence you play.
RUTH. I'm not the one to plot so.
FRED. Your face is lined, your hair is grey.
RUTH. It's gradually got so.
FRED. Faithless woman, to deceive me,
I who trusted so!
RUTH. Master, master, do not leave me!
Hear me, ere you go!
My love without reflecting,
Oh, do not be rejecting.
Take a maiden tender—her affection raw and green,
At very highest rating,
Has been accumulating
Summers seventeen—summers seventeen.
Don't, beloved master,
Crush me with disaster.
What is such a dower to the dower I have here?
My love unabating
Has been accumulating
Forty-seven year—forty-seven year!

ENSEMBLE

RUTH	FRED.
Don't, beloved master,	Yes, your former master
Crush me with disaster.	Saves you from disaster.
What is such a dower to the dower I have here?	Your love would be uncomfortably fervid, it is clear,
My love unabating	If, as you are stating,
Has been accumulating	It's been accumulating
Forty-seven year—forty-seven year!	Forty-seven year—forty-seven year!

[At the end he renounces her, and she goes off in despair.

RECITATIVE—FRED.

What shall I do? Before these gentle maidens
I dare not show in this alarming costume.
No, no, I must remain in close concealment
Until I can appear in decent clothing!

(*Hides in cave as they enter climbing over the rocks.*)

GIRLS. Climbing over rocky mountain,
  Skipping rivulet and fountain,
  Passing where the willows quiver
  By the ever-rolling river,
   Swollen with the summer rain;
  Threading long and leafy mazes
  Dotted with unnumbered daisies;
  Scaling rough and rugged passes,
  Climb the hardy little lasses,
   Till the bright sea-shore they gain!

EDITH. Let us gaily tread the measure,
  Make the most of fleeting leisure;
  Hail it as a true ally,
  Though it perish by and by.

ALL. Hail it as a true ally,
  Though it perish by and by.

EDITH. Every moment brings a treasure
  Of its own especial pleasure,
  Though the moments quickly die,
  Greet them gaily as they fly.

KATE. Far away from toil and care,
  Revelling in fresh sea air,
  Here we live and reign alone
  In a world that's all our own.
  Here in this our rocky den,
  Far away from mortal men,
  We'll be queens, and make decrees—
  They may honour them who please.

ALL. Let us gaily tread the measure, etc.

KATE. What a picturesque spot! I wonder where we are!

EDITH. And I wonder where papa is. We have left him ever so far behind.

ISABEL. Oh, he will be here presently! Remember poor papa is not as young as we are, and we have come over a rather difficult country.

KATE. But how thoroughly delightful it is to be so entirely alone! Why, in all probability we are the first human beings who ever set foot on this enchanting spot.

ISABEL. Except the mermaids—it's the very place for mermaids.

KATE. Who are only human beings down to the waist!

EDITH. And who can't be said strictly to set *foot* anywhere. Tails they may, but feet they *cannot.*

KATE. But what shall we do until papa and the servants arrive with the luncheon?

EDITH. We are quite alone, and the sea is as smooth as glass. Suppose we take off our shoes and stockings and paddle?

ALL. Yes, yes! The very thing! (*They prepare to carry out the suggestion. They have all taken off one shoe, when* FREDERIC *comes forward from cave.*)

RECITATIVE—FRED. *with* GIRLS

FRED. Stop, ladies, pray!
ALL (*hopping on one foot*). A man!
FRED.   I had intended
  Not to intrude myself upon your notice
  In this effective but alarming costume,
  But under these peculiar circumstances
  It is my bounden duty to inform you
  That your proceedings will not be unwitnessed!
EDITH. But who are you, sir? Speak! (*All hopping.*)
FRED.   I am a pirate!
ALL (*recoiling, hopping*). A pirate! Horror!
FRED.   Ladies, do not shun me!
  This evening I renounce my wild profession;
  And to that end, oh, pure and peerless maidens!
  Oh, blushing buds of ever-blooming beauty!
  I, sore at heart, implore your kind assistance.
EDITH. How pitiful his tale!
KATE.   How rare his beauty!
ALL. How pitiful his tale! How rare his beauty!

SONG—FRED.

  Oh, is there not one maiden breast
   Which does not feel the moral beauty
  Of making worldly interest
   Subordinate to sense of duty?
  Who would not give up willingly
   All matrimonial ambition,
  To rescue such a one as I
   From his unfortunate position?

ALL. Alas! there's not one maiden breast
   Which seems to feel the moral beauty
  Of making worldly interest
   Subordinate to sense of duty!

FRED. Oh, is there not one maiden here
   Whose homely face and bad complexion
  Have caused all hopes to disappear
   Of ever winning man's affection?
  To such a one, if such there be,
   I swear by Heaven's arch above you,
  If you will cast your eyes on me—
   However plain you be—I'll love you!

ALL. Alas! there's not one maiden here
   Whose homely face and bad complexion
  Have caused all hope to disappear
   Of ever winning man's affection!

FRED. (*in despair*). Not one?

ALL. No, no—not one!

FRED. Not one?

ALL. No, no!

MABEL *enters*

MABEL. Yes, one!

ALL. 'Tis Mabel!

MABEL. Yes, 'tis Mabel!

RECITATIVE—MABEL

Oh, sisters, deaf to pity's name,
For shame!
It's true that he has gone astray,
But pray
Is that a reason good and true
Why you
Should all be deaf to pity's name?

ALL (*aside*). The question is, had he not been
A thing of beauty,
Would she be swayed by quite as keen
A sense of duty?

MABEL. For shame, for shame, for shame!

SONG—MABEL

Poor wandering one!
Though thou hast surely strayed,
Take heart of grace,
Thy steps retrace,
Poor wandering one!
Poor wandering one!
If such poor love as mine
Can help thee find
True peace of mind—
Why, take it, it is thine!
Take heart, fair days will shine;
Take any heart—take mine!

ALL. Take heart; no danger lowers;
Take any heart—but ours!

[*Exeunt* MABEL *and* FREDERIC.

(EDITH *beckons her sisters, who form in a semicircle
around her.*)

EDITH

What ought we to do,
Gentle sisters, say?
Propriety, we know,
Says we ought to stay;
While sympathy exclaims,
"Free them from your tether—
Play at other games—
Leave them here together."

KATE

Her case may, any day,
Be yours, my dear, or mine.
Let her make her hay
While the sun doth shine.
Let us compromise,
(Our hearts are not of leather.)
Let us shut our eyes,
And talk about the weather.

GIRLS. Yes, yes, let's talk about the weather.
Chattering chorus
How beautifully blue the sky,
The glass is rising very high,
Continue fine I hope it may,
And yet it rained but yesterday.
To-morrow it may pour again
(I hear the country wants some rain),
Yet people say, I know not why,
That we shall have a warm July.

Enter MABEL *and* FREDERIC

[*During* MABEL'S *solo the* GIRLS *continue chatter
pianissimo, but listening eagerly all the time.*

SOLO—MABEL

Did ever maiden wake
From dream of homely duty,
To find her daylight break
With such exceeding beauty?
Did ever maiden close
Her eyes on waking sadness,
To dream of such exceeding gladness?

FRED. Oh, yes! ah, yes! this is exceeding gladness.

GIRLS. How beautifully blue the sky, etc.

SOLO—FRED.

[*During this,* GIRLS *continue their chatter pianissimo
as before, but listening intently all the time.*

Did ever pirate roll
His soul in guilty dreaming,
And wake to find that soul
With peace and virtue beaming?

ENSEMBLE

MABEL	FRED.	GIRLS
Did ever maiden wake, etc.	Did ever pirate roll, etc.	How beautifully blue the sky, etc.

RECITATIVE—FRED.

Stay, we must not lose our senses;
Men who stick at no offences
Will anon be here.
Piracy their dreadful trade is

So I made up my mind to go as a kind of piratical maid-of-all-work.

> Pray you, get you hence, young ladies,
> While the coast is clear.
> [FREDERICK *and* MABEL *retire.*

GIRLS. No, we must not lose our senses,
If they stick at no offences
We should not be here.
Piracy their dreadful trade is—
Nice companions for the young ladies!
Let us disappear.

[*During this chorus the* PIRATES *have entered stealthily, and formed in a semicircle behind the* GIRLS. *As the* GIRLS *move to go off each* PIRATE *seizes a girl.* KING *seizes* EDITH *and* ISABEL, SAMUEL *seizes* KATE.

ALL.   Too late!
PIRATES.   Ha! Ha!
ALL.   Too late!
PIRATES.   Ha! Ha!
Ha! ha! ha! ha!   Ha! ha! ha! ha!

ENSEMBLE

(*Pirates pass in front of Girls.*)   (*Girls pass in front of Pirates.*)

PIRATES	GIRLS
Here's a first-rate opportunity	We have missed our opportunity
To get married with impunity,	Of escaping with impunity;
And indulge in the felicity	So farewell to the felicity
Of unbounded domesticity.	Of our maiden domesticity!
You shall quickly be parsonified,	We shall quickly be parsonified,
Conjugally matrimonified,	Conjugally matrimonified,
By a doctor of divinity,	By a doctor of divinity,
Who resides in this vicinity.	Who resides in this vicinity.

MABEL (*coming forward*).

RECITATIVE—MABEL

Hold, monsters! Ere your pirate caravanserai
Proceed, against our will, to wed us all,
Just bear in mind that we are Wards in Chancery,
And father is a Major-General!

SAM. (*cowed*). We'd better pause, or danger may befall,
Their father is a Major-General.

GIRLS. Yes, yes; he is a Major-General!

The MAJOR-GENERAL *has entered unnoticed, on rock*

GEN.   Yes, I am a Major-General!
SAM.   For he is a Major-General!
ALL.   He is! Hurrah for the Major-General!
GEN.   And it is—it is a glorious thing
To be a Major-General!
ALL.   It is! Hurrah for the Major-General!

SONG—MAJOR-GENERAL

I am the very model of a modern Major-General,
I've information vegetable, animal, and mineral,

I know the kings of England, and I quote the fights historical,
From Marathon to Waterloo, in order categorical;
I'm very well acquainted too with matters mathematical,
I understand equations, both the simple and quadratical,
About binomial theorem I'm teeming with a lot o' news—
With many cheerful facts about the square of the hypotenuse.

ALL. With many cheerful facts, etc.

GEN. I'm very good at integral and differential calculus,
I know the scientific names of beings animalculous;
In short, in matters vegetable, animal, and mineral,
I am the very model of a modern Major-General.

ALL. In short, in matters vegetable, animal, and mineral,
He is the very model of a modern Major-General.

GEN. I know our mythic history, King Arthur's and Sir Caradoc's,
I answer hard acrostics, I've a pretty taste for paradox,
I quote in elegiacs all the crimes of Heliogabalus,
In conics I can floor peculiarities parabolous.
I can tell undoubted Raphaels from Gerard Dows and Zoffanys,
I know the croaking chorus from the *Frogs* of Aristophanes,
Then I can hum a fugue of which I've heard the music's din afore,
And whistle all the airs from that infernal nonsense *Pinafore.*

ALL. And whistle all the airs, etc.

GEN. Then I can write a washing bill in Babylonic cuneiform,
And tell you every detail of Caractacus's uniform;
In short, in matters vegetable, animal, and mineral,
I am the very model of a modern Major-General.

ALL. In short, in matters vegetable, animal, and mineral,
He is the very model of a modern Major-General.

GEN. In fact, when I know what is meant by "mamelon" and "ravelin,"
When I can tell at sight a chassepot rifle from a javelin,
When such affairs as sorties and surprises I'm more wary at,
And when I know precisely what is meant by "commissariat,"
When I have learnt what progress has been made in modern gunnery,
When I know more of tactics than a novice in a nunnery:

In short, when I've a smattering of elemental strategy,
You'll say a better Major-Gener*al* has never *sat a gee—*

ALL. You'll say a better, etc.

GEN. For my military knowledge, though I'm plucky and
      adventury,
Has only been brought down to the beginning of the
      century;
But still in matters vegetable, animal, and mineral,
I am the very model of a modern Major-General.

ALL. But still in matters vegetable, animal, and mineral,
He is the very model of a modern Major-General.

GEN. And now that I've introduced myself I should like to
have some idea of what's going on.

KATE. Oh, papa—we—

SAM. Permit me, I'll explain in two words: we propose to
marry your daughters.

GEN. Dear me!

GIRLS. Against our wills, papa—against our wills!

GEN. Oh, but you mustn't do that! May I ask—this is a
picturesque uniform, but I'm not familiar with it. What are
you?

KING. We are all single gentlemen.

GEN. Yes, I gathered that—anything else?

KING. No, nothing else.

EDITH. Papa, don't believe them; they are pirates—the fa-
mous Pirates of Penzance!

GEN. The Pirates of Penzance! I have often heard of them.

MABEL. All except this gentleman—(*indicating* FREDERIC)—
who was a pirate once, but who is out of his indentures to-
day, and who means to lead a blameless life evermore.

GEN. But wait a bit. I object to pirates as sons-in-law.

KING. We object to Major-Generals as fathers-in-law. But
we waive that point. We do not press it. We look over it.

GEN. (*aside*). Hah! an idea! (*Aloud.*) And do you mean to
say that you would deliberately rob me of these, the sole
remaining props of my old age, and leave me to go through
the remainder of my life unfriended, unprotected, and alone?

KING. Well, yes, that's the idea.

GEN. Tell me, have you ever known what it is to be an
orphan?

PIRATES (*disgusted*). Oh, dash it all!

KING. Here we are again!

GEN. I ask you, have you ever known what it is to be an
orphan?

KING. Often!

GEN. Yes, orphan. Have you ever known what it is to be
one?

KING. I say, often.

ALL (*disgusted*). Often, often, often. (*Turning away.*)

GEN. I don't think we quite understand one another. I ask
you, have you ever known what it is to be an orphan, and you
say "orphan." As I understand you, you are merely repeating
the word "orphan" to show that you understand me.

KING. I didn't repeat the word often.

GEN. Pardon me, you did indeed.

KING. I only repeated it once.

GEN. True, but you repeated it.

KING. But not often.

GEN. Stop: I think I see where we are getting confused.
When you said "orphan," did you mean "orphan"—a person
who has lost his parents, or "often"—frequently?

KING. Ah! I beg pardon—I see what you mean—frequently.

GEN. Ah! you said often—frequently.

KING. No, only once.

GEN. (*irritated*). Exactly—you said often, frequently, only
once.

RECITATIVE—GENERAL

Oh, men of dark and dismal fate,
    Forgo your cruel employ,
Have pity on my lonely state,
    I am an orphan boy!

KING *and* SAM.   An orphan boy?
GEN.   An orphan boy!
PIRATES.   How sad—an orphan boy.

SOLO—GENERAL

These children whom you see
    Are all that I can call my own!
PIRATES.   Poor fellow!
GEN.   Take them away from me
    And I shall be indeed alone.
PIRATES.   Poor fellow!
GEN.   If pity you can feel,
    Leave me my sole remaining joy—
    See, at your feet they kneel;
    Your hearts you cannot steel
Against the sad, sad tale of the lonely orphan boy!
PIRATES (*sobbing*).   Poor fellow!
    See at our feet they kneel;
    Our hearts we cannot steel
Against the sad, sad tale of the lonely orphan boy!
KING. The orphan boy!
SAM.   The orphan boy!
ALL.   The lonely orphan boy! Poor fellow!

ENSEMBLE

GENERAL (*aside*)	GIRLS (*aside*)	PIRATES (*aside*)
I'm telling a terrible story	He's telling a terrible story,	If he's telling a terrible story,
But it doesn't dimin-ish my glory;	Which will tend to di-minish his glory;	He shall die by a death that is gory,
For they would have taken my daughters	Though they would have taken his daughters	One of the cruellest slaughters
Over the billowy wa-ters,	Over the billowy wa-ters.	That ever were known in these waters;
If I hadn't, in elegant diction,	It's easy, in elegant diction,	And we'll finish his moral affliction

Indulged in an inno-
cent fiction;
Which is not in the
same category
As a regular terrible
story.

To call it an innocent
fiction,
But it comes in the
same category
As a regular terrible
story.

By a very complete
malediction,
As a compliment vale-
dictory,
If he's telling a terrible
story.

KING.   Although our dark career
      Sometimes involves the crime of stealing,
    We rather think that we're
      Not altogether void of feeling.
    Although we live by strife,
      We're always sorry to begin it,
    For what, we ask, is life
      Without a touch of Poetry in it?

ALL (*kneeling*).
    Hail, Poetry, thou heaven-born maid!
    Thou gildest e'en the pirate's trade:
    Hail, flowing fount of sentiment!
    All hail, Divine Emollient! (*All rise.*)

KING.   You may go, for you're at liberty, our pirate rules
      protect you,
    And honorary members of our band we do elect
      you!

SAM.   For he is an orphan boy.

CHORUS.   He is! Hurrah for the orphan boy.
GEN.   And it sometimes is a useful thing
      To be an orphan boy.
CHORUS.   It is! Hurrah for the orphan boy!

    Oh, happy day, with joyous glee
    They will away and married be;
    Should it befall auspiciously,
    Our sisters all will bridesmaids be!

RUTH *enters and comes down to* FREDERIC

RUTH.   Oh, master, hear one word, I do implore you!
    Remember Ruth, your Ruth, who kneels before
      you!
CHORUS.   Yes, yes, remember Ruth, who kneels before you!
FRED.   (PIRATES *threaten* RUTH.) Away, you did deceive
      me!
CHORUS.   Away, you did deceive him!

RUTH.   Oh, do not leave me!
CHORUS.   Oh, do not leave her!

FRED.   Away, you grieve me!
CHORUS.   Away, you grieve him!
FRED.   I wish you'd leave me!

    (FREDERIC *casts* RUTH *from him.*)

CHORUS.   We wish you'd leave him!

ENSEMBLE

Pray observe the magnanimity
We ⎫
They ⎭ display to lace and dimity!
Never was such opportunity
To get married with impunity,
But ⎧ we ⎫ give up the felicity
    ⎩ they ⎭
Of unbounded domesticity,
Though a doctor of divinity
Resides in this vicinity.

[GIRLS *and* GENERAL *go up rocks, while* PIRATES
indulge in a wild dance of delight on stage. The
GENERAL *produces a British flag, and the* PIRATE
KING *produces a black flag with skull and cross-*
bones. Enter RUTH, *who makes a final appeal to*
FREDERIC, *who casts her from him.*

END OF ACT I

ACT II

SCENE.—*A Ruined Chapel by Moonlight. Ruined Gothic windows*
at back. GENERAL STANLEY *discovered seated pensively, sur-*
rounded by his daughters.

CHORUS

Oh, dry the glistening tear
    That dews that martial cheek;
Thy loving children hear,
    In them thy comfort seek.
With sympathetic care
    Their arms around thee creep,
For oh, they cannot bear
    To see their father weep!

Enter MABEL

SOLO—MABEL

Dear father, why leave your bed
    At this untimely hour,
When happy daylight is dead,
    And darksome dangers lower?
See heaven has lit her lamp,
    The midnight hour is past,
The chilly night air is damp,
    And the dews are falling fast!
Dear father, why leave your bed
When happy daylight is dead?

FREDERIC *enters*

Hurrah for our Pirate King!

MABEL. Oh, Frederic, cannot you, in the calm excellence of your wisdom, reconcile it with your conscience to say something that will relieve my father's sorrow?

FRED. I will try, dear Mabel. But why does he sit, night after night, in this draughty old ruin?

GEN. Why do I sit here? To escape from the pirates' clutches, I described myself as an orphan, and, heaven help me, I am no orphan! I come here to humble myself before the tombs of my ancestors, and to implore their pardon for having brought dishonour on the family escutcheon.

FRED. But you forget, sir, you only bought the property a year ago, and the stucco in your baronial hall is scarcely dry.

GEN. Frederic, in this chapel are ancestors: you cannot deny that. With the estate, I bought the chapel and its contents. I don't know whose ancestors they *were,* but I know whose ancestors they *are,* and I shudder to think that their descendant by purchase (if I may so describe myself) should have brought disgrace upon what, I have no doubt, was an unstained escutcheon.

FRED. Be comforted. Had you not acted as you did, these reckless men would assuredly have called in the nearest clergyman, and have married your large family on the spot.

GEN. I thank you for your proffered solace, but it is unavailing. I assure you, Frederic, that such is the anguish and remorse I feel at the abominable falsehood by which I escaped these easily deluded pirates, that I would go to their simpleminded chief this very night and confess all, did I not fear that the consequences would be most disastrous to myself. At what time does your expedition march against these scoundrels?

FRED. At eleven, and before midnight I hope to have atoned for my involuntary association with the pestilent scourges by sweeping them from the face of the earth—and then, dear Mabel, you will be mine!

GEN. Are your devoted followers at hand?

FRED. They are, they only wait my orders.

RECITATIVE—GENERAL

Then, Frederic, let your escort lion-hearted
Be summoned to receive a General's blessing,
Ere they depart upon their dread adventure.

FRED. Dear sir, they come.

Enter POLICE, *marching in single file. They form in line, facing audience*

SONG—SERGEANT

When the foeman bares his steel,
   Tarantara! tarantara!
We uncomfortable feel,
   Tarantara!
And we find the wisest thing,
   Tarantara! tarantara!
Is to slap our chests and sing
   Tarantara!

For when threatened with émeutes,
   Tarantara! tarantara!
And your heart is in your boots,
   Tarantara!
There is nothing brings it round,
   Tarantara! tarantara!
Like the trumpet's martial sound,
   Tarantara! tarantara!

Tarantara-ra-ra-ra-ra!

ALL. Tarantara-ra-ra-ra-ra!

MABEL. Go, ye heroes, go to glory,
Though you die in combat gory,
Ye shall live in song and story.
  Go to immortality!
Go to death, and go to slaughter;
Die, and every Cornish daughter
With her tears your grave shall water.
  Go, ye heroes, go and die!

ALL.   Go, ye heroes, go and die!

POLICE. Though to us it's evident,
   Tarantara! tarantara!
These intentions are well meant,
   Tarantara!
Such expressions don't appear,
   Tarantara! tarantara!
Calculated men to cheer,
   Tarantara!
Who are going to meet their fate
In a highly nervous state,
   Tarantara!
Still to us it's evident
These intentions are well meant.
   Tarantara!

EDITH. Go and do your best endeavour,
And before all links we sever,
We will say farewell for ever.
  Go to glory and the grave!

GIRLS. For your foes are fierce and ruthless,
False, unmerciful, and truthless.
Young and tender, old and toothless,
  All in vain their mercy crave.

SERG. We observe too great a stress,
On the risks that on us press,
And of reference a lack
To our chance of coming back.
Still, perhaps it would be wise
Not to carp or criticise,
For it's very evident
These attentions are well meant.

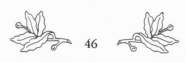

ALL.   Yes, to them it's evident
        Our attentions are well meant.
                  Tarantara-ra-ra-ra-ra!

        Go, ye heroes, go to glory, etc.

ENSEMBLE

Chorus of all but Police	*Chorus of Police*
Go and do your best endeavour,	Such expressions don't appear,
And before all links we sever,	Tarantara, tarantara!
We will say farewell for ever.	Calculated men to cheer,
Go to glory and the grave!	Tarantara!
For your foes are fierce and ruthless,	Who are going to their fate,
False, unmerciful, and truthless.	Tarantara, tarantara!
Young and tender, old and tooth-	In a highly nervous state—
less,	Tarantara!
All in vain their mercy crave.	We observe too great a stress,
	Tarantara, tarantara!
	On the risks that on us press,
	Tarantara!
	And of reference a lack,
	Tarantara, tarantara!
	To our chance of coming back,
	Tarantara!

GEN.   Away, away!
POLICE (*without moving*).   Yes, yes, we go.
GEN.   These pirates slay.
POLICE.   Tarantara!
GEN.   Then do not stay.
POLICE.   Tarantara!
GEN.   Then why this delay?
POLICE.   All right—we go.
         Yes, forward on the foe!
GIRLS.   Yes, but you *don't* go!
POLICE.   We go, we go!
         Yes, forward on the foe!
GEN.   Yes, but you *don't* go!
ALL.   At last they really go.

[MABEL *tears herself from* FREDERIC *and exits, followed by her sisters, consoling her. The* GENERAL *and others follow.* FREDERIC *remains.*

RECITATIVE—FRED.

Now for the pirates' lair! Oh, joy unbounded!
Oh, sweet relief! Oh, rapture unexampled!
At last I may atone, in some slight measure,
For the repeated acts of theft and pillage
Which, at a sense of duty's stern dictation,
I, circumstance's victim, have been guilty.

(KING *and* RUTH *appear at the window, armed.*)

KING.   Young Frederic! (*Covering him with pistol.*)
FRED.   Who calls?
KING.   Your late commander!
RUTH.   And I, your little Ruth! (*Covering him with pistol.*)
FRED.   Oh, mad intruders,

How dare ye face me? Know ye not, oh rash ones,
That I have doomed you to extermination?

(KING *and* RUTH *hold a pistol to each ear.*)

KING.   Have mercy on us, hear us, ere you slaughter.
FRED.   I do not think I ought to listen to you.
        Yet, mercy should alloy our stern resentment,
        And so I will be merciful—say on!

TRIO—RUTH, KING, *and* FRED.

RUTH.   When you had left our pirate fold
        We tried to raise our spirits faint,
    According to our customs old,
        With quips and quibbles quaint.
    But all in vain the quips we heard,
        We lay and sobbed upon the rocks,
    Until to somebody occurred
        A startling paradox.
FRED.   A paradox?
KING (*laughing*).   A paradox!
RUTH.   A most ingenious paradox!
    We've quips and quibbles heard in flocks,
    But none to beat this paradox!
      Ha! ha! ha! ha! Ho! ho! ho! ho!
KING.   We knew your taste for curious quips,
        For cranks and contradictions queer,
    And with the laughter on our lips,
        We wished you there to hear.
    We said, "If we could tell it him,
        How Frederic would the joke enjoy!"
    And so we've risked both life and limb
        To tell it to our boy.
FRED. (*interested*). That paradox? That paradox?
KING
and   (*laughing*). That most ingenious paradox!
RUTH

    We've quips and quibbles heard in flocks,
    But none to beat that paradox!
      Ha! ha! ha! ha! Ho! ho! ho! ho!

CHANT—KING

For some ridiculous reason, to which, however, I've no desire
    to be disloyal,
Some person in authority, I don't know who, very likely the
    Astronomer Royal,
Has decided that, although for such a beastly month as Febru-
    ary, twenty-eight days as a rule are plenty,
One year in every four his days shall be reckoned as nine-and-
    twenty.
Through some singular coincidence—I shouldn't be surprised
    if it were owing to the agency of an ill-natured fairy—
You are the victim of this clumsy arrangement, having been
    born in leap-year, on the twenty-ninth of February,
And so, by a simple arithmetical process, you'll easily discover,

That though you've lived twenty-one years, yet, if we go by
    birthdays, you're only five and a little bit over!

RUTH.   Ha! ha! ha! ha!

KING.   Ho! ho! ho! ho!

FRED.   Dear me!
            Let's see! (*counting on fingers*).
            Yes, yes; with yours my figures do agree!

ALL.   Ha! ha! ha! ha! Ho! ho! ho! ho! (FREDERIC *more*
            amused than any.)

FRED.   How quaint the ways of Paradox!
            At common sense she gaily mocks!
            Though counting in the usual way,
                Years twenty-one I've been alive,
            Yet, reckoning by my natal day,
            I am a little boy of five!

ALL.   He is a little boy of five! Ha! ha!
            A paradox, a paradox,
            A most ingenious paradox!
            Ha! ha! ha! ha! Ho! ho! ho! ho! (RUTH *and*
            KING *throw themselves back on seats, exhausted*
            with laughter.)

FRED. Upon my word, this is most curious—most absurdly
whimsical. Five-and-a-quarter! No one would think it to look
at me!

RUTH. You are glad now, I'll be bound, that you spared us.
You would never have forgiven yourself when you discovered
that you had killed *two of your comrades.*

FRED. My comrades?

KING (*rises*). I'm afraid you don't appreciate the delicacy of
your position. You were apprenticed to us—

FRED. Until I reached my twenty-first year.

KING. No, until you reached your twenty-first *birthday*
(*producing document*), and, going by birthdays, you are as yet
only five-and-a-quarter.

FRED. You don't mean to say you are going to hold me to
that?

KING. No, we merely remind you of the fact, and leave the
rest to your sense of duty.

RUTH. Your sense of duty!

FRED. (*wildly*). Don't put it on that footing! As I was
merciful to you just now, be merciful to me! I implore you
not to insist on the letter of your bond just as the cup of
happiness is at my lips!

RUTH. We insist on nothing; we content ourselves with
pointing out to you *your duty.*

KING. Your duty!

FRED. (*after a pause*). Well, you have appealed to my sense
of duty, and my duty is only too clear. I abhor your infamous
calling; I shudder at the thought that I have ever been mixed
up with it; but duty is before all—at any price I will do my
duty.

KING. Bravely spoken! Come, you are one of us once more.

FRED. Lead on, I follow. (*Suddenly.*) Oh, horror!

KING.
RUTH. } What is the matter?

FRED. Ought I to tell you? No, no, I cannot do it; and yet,
as one of your band—

KING. Speak out, I charge you by that sense of conscientiousness to which we have never yet appealed in vain.

FRED. General Stanley, the father of my Mabel—

KING.
RUTH. } Yes, yes!

FRED. He escaped from you on the plea that he was an
orphan!

KING. He did!

FRED. It breaks my heart to betray the honoured father of
the girl I adore, but as your apprentice I have no alternative.
It is my duty to tell you that General Stanley is no orphan!

KING.
RUTH. } What!

FRED. More than that, he never was one!

KING. Am I to understand that, to save his contemptible
life, he dared to practise on our credulous simplicity? (FRED-
ERIC *nods as he weeps.*) Our revenge shall be swift and terrible.
We will go and collect our band and attack Tremorden Castle
this very night.

FRED. But—stay—

KING. Not a word! He is doomed!

TRIO

KING *and* RUTH	FRED.
Away, away! my heart's on fire,	Away, away! ere I expire—
I burn this base deception to	I find my duty hard to do to day!
repay,	
This very night my vengeance dire	My heart is filled with anguish dire,
Shall glut itself in gore. Away,	It strikes me to the core. Away,
away!	away!

KING.   With falsehood foul
            He tricked us of our brides.
                Let vengeance howl;
            The Pirate so decides.
                Our nature stern
            He softened with his lies,
                And, in return,
            To-night the traitor dies.

ALL.   Yes, yes! to-night the traitor dies.

RUTH.   To-night he dies!

KING.   Yes, or early to-morrow.

FRED.   His girls likewise?

RUTH.   They will welter in sorrow.

KING.   The one soft spot

FRED.   In their natures they cherish—

RUTH.   And all who plot

KING.   To abuse it shall perish!

ALL.   Yes, all who plot
            To abuse it shall perish!
            Away, away! etc.

[*Exeunt* KING *and* RUTH.

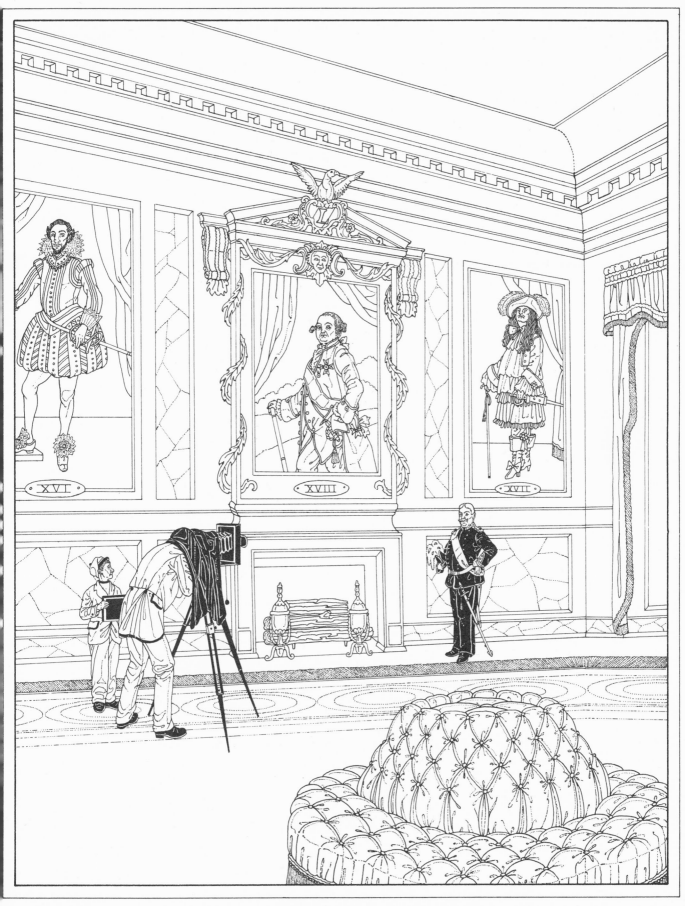

I am the very model of a modern Major-General, . . .

Enter MABEL

RECITATIVE—MABEL

All is prepared, your gallant crew await you.
My Frederic in tears? It cannot be
That lion-heart quails at the coming conflict?

FRED. No, Mabel, no. A terrible disclosure
Has just been made! Mabel, my dearly-loved one,
I bound myself to serve the pirate captain
Until I reached my one-and-twentieth birthday—
MABEL. But you *are* twenty-one?
FRED.   I've just discovered
That I was born in leap-year, and that birthday
Will not be reached by me till 1940.
MABEL. Oh, horrible! catastrophe appalling!
FRED. And so, farewell!
MABEL. No, no! Ah, Frederic, hear me.

DUET—MABEL *and* FRED.

MABEL.   Stay, Frederic, stay!
                They have no legal claim,
                No shadow of a shame
                Will fall upon thy name.
            Stay, Frederic, stay!

FRED.   Nay, Mabel, nay!
                To-night I quit these walls,
                The thought my soul appals,
                But when stern Duty calls,
            I must obey.

MABEL.   Stay, Frederic, stay!
FRED.   Nay, Mabel, nay!
MABEL.   They have no claim—
FRED.   But Duty's name!
            The thought my soul appals,
            But when stern Duty calls,
        I must obey.

BALLAD—MABEL

Ah, leave me not to pine
    Alone and desolate;
No fate seemed fair as mine,
    No happiness so great!
And nature, day by day,
    Has sung, in accents clear,
This joyous roundelay,
    "He loves thee—he is here.
        Fa-la, fa-la, fa-la."

FRED.   Ah, must I leave thee here
            In endless night to dream,
        Where joy is dark and drear,
            And sorrow all supreme!

Where nature, day by day,
    Will sing, in altered tone,
This weary roundelay,
    "He loves thee—he is gone.
        Fa-la, fa-la, fa-la."

FRED. In 1940 I of age shall be,
I'll then return, and claim you—I declare it!
MABEL.   It seems so long!
FRED. Swear that, till then, you will be true to me.
MABEL.   Yes, I'll be strong!
By all the Stanleys dead and gone, I swear it!

ENSEMBLE

Oh, here is love, and here is truth,
    And here is food for joyous laughter.
He | will be faithful to | his | sooth
She | | her |
Till we are wed, and even after.

[FREDERIC *rushes to window and leaps out.*

MABEL (*almost fainting*). No, I am brave! Oh, family descent,
How great thy charm, thy sway how excellent!
Come, one and all, undaunted men in blue,
A crisis, now, affairs are coming to!

Enter Police, marching in single file

SERG.   Though in body and in mind,
                Tarantara, tarantara!
            We are timidly inclined,
                Tarantara!
            And anything but blind,
                Tarantara, tarantara!
            To the danger that's behind,
                Tarantara!
            Yet, when the danger's near,
                Tarantara, tarantara!
            We manage to appear,
                Tarantara!
            As insensible to fear
            As anybody here.
                Tarantara, tarantara-ra-ra-ra-ra!

MABEL. Sergeant, approach! Young Frederic was to have led you to death and glory.

ALL. That is not a pleasant way of putting it.

MABEL. No matter; he will not so lead you, for he has allied himself once more with his old associates.

ALL. He has acted shamefully!

MABEL. You speak falsely. You know nothing about it. He has acted nobly.

ALL. He has acted nobly!

MABEL. Dearly as I loved him before, his heroic sacrifice to his sense of duty has endeared him to me tenfold. He has done his duty. I will do mine. Go ye and do yours.

[*Exit* MABEL.

ALL. Right oh!

SERG. This is perplexing.

ALL. We cannot understand it at all.

SERG. Still, as he is actuated by a sense of duty—

ALL. That makes a difference, of course. At the same time we repeat, we cannot understand it at all.

SERG. No matter; our course is clear. We must do our best to capture these pirates alone. It is most distressing to us to be the agents whereby our erring fellow-creatures are deprived of that liberty which is so dear to all—but we should have thought of that before we joined the Force.

ALL. We should!

SERG. It is too late now!

ALL. It is!

SONG—SERGEANT

SERG. When a felon's not engaged in his employment—

ALL.   His employment,

SERG. Or maturing his felonious little plans—

ALL.   Little plans,

SERG. His capacity for innocent enjoyment—

ALL.   'Cent enjoyment

SERG. Is just as great as any honest man's—

ALL.   Honest man's.

SERG. Our feelings we with difficulty smother—

ALL.   'Culty smother

SERG. When constabulary duty's to be done—

ALL.   To be done.

SERG. Ah, take one consideration with another—

ALL.   With another,

SERG. A policeman's lot is not a happy one.

ALL.   When constabulary duty's to be done—
            To be done,
      The policeman's lot is not a happy one.

SERG. When the enterprising burglar's not a-burgling—

ALL.   Not a-burgling,

SERG. When the cut-throat isn't occupied in crime

ALL.   'Pied in crime,

SERG. He loves to hear the little brook a-gurgling—

ALL.   Brook a-gurgling,

SERG. And listen to the merry village chime—

ALL.   Village chime.

SERG. When the coster's finished jumping on his mother—

ALL.   On his mother,

SERG. He loves to lie a-basking in the sun—

ALL.   In the sun.

SERG. Ah, take one consideration with another—

ALL.   With another,

SERG. The policeman's lot is not a happy one.

ALL.   When constabulary duty's to be done—
            To be done,
      The policeman's lot is not a happy one—
            Happy one.

(*Chorus of Pirates without, in the distance.*)

     A rollicking band of pirates we,
       Who, tired of tossing on the sea,
       Are trying their hand at a burglaree,
         With weapons grim and gory.

SERG. Hush, hush! I hear them on the manor poaching,
      With stealthy step the pirates are approaching.

(*Chorus of Pirates, resumed nearer.*)

      We are not coming for plate or gold—
      A story General Stanley's told—
      We seek a penalty fifty-fold,
        For General Stanley's story.

POLICE.   They seek a penalty—

PIRATES (*without*).   Fifty-fold,
      We seek a penalty—

POLICE.   Fifty-fold.

ALL.   We ⎱ seek a penalty fifty-fold,
       They ⎰

      For General Stanley's story.

SERG.   They come in force, with stealthy stride,
      Our obvious course is now—to hide.

[*Police conceal themselves. As they do so, the Pirates are seen appearing at ruined window. They enter cautiously, and come down stage.* SAMUEL *is laden with burglarious tools and pistols, etc.*

CHORUS—PIRATES (*very loud*)

     With cat-like tread,
       Upon our prey we steal,
     In silence dread
       Our cautious way we feel.
     No sound at all,
       We never speak a word,
     A fly's foot-fall
       Would be distinctly heard—

POLICE (*pianissimo*).   Tarantara, tarantara!

PIRATES.   So stealthily the pirate creeps,
      While all the household soundly sleeps.
      Come, friends, who plough the sea,
       Truce to navigation,
       Take another station;
      Let's vary piracee
      With a little burglaree!

POLICE (*pianissimo*).   Tarantara, tarantara!

SAM. (*distributing implements to various members of the gang*).
      Here's your crowbar and your centrebit,
      Your life-preserver—you may want to hit;
      Your silent matches, your dark lantern seize,
      Take your file and your skeletonic keys.

Enter KING, FREDERIC, *and* RUTH

ALL (*fortissimo*). With cat-like tread, etc.

RECITATIVE—FRED. *with others*

FRED. Hush, hush, not a word! I see a light inside!
The Major-General comes, so quickly hide!

PIRATES. Yes, yes, the Major-General comes!

[*Exeunt* KING, FREDERIC, SAMUEL, *and* RUTH.

POLICE. Yes, yes, the Major-General comes!

GEN. (*entering in dressing-gown, carrying a light*).
Yes, yes, the Major-General comes!

SOLO—GENERAL

Tormented with the anguish dread
Of falsehood unatoned,
I lay upon my sleepless bed,
And tossed and turned and groaned.
The man who finds his conscience ache
No peace at all enjoys,
And as I lay in bed awake
I thought I heard a noise.

PIRATES. } He thought he heard a noise—ha! ha!
POLICE. } He thought he heard a noise—ha! ha! (*Very loud.*)

GEN. No, all is still
In dale, on hill;
My mind is set at ease.
So still the scene—
It must have been
The sighing of the breeze.

BALLAD—GENERAL

Sighing softly to the river
Comes the loving breeze,
Setting nature all a-quiver,
Rustling through the trees—

ALL. Through the trees.

GEN. And the brook, in rippling measure,
Laughs for very love,
While the poplars, in their pleasure,
Wave their arms above.

POLICE. } Yes, the trees, for very love,
and } Wave their leafy arms above.
PIRATES. } River, river, little river,
May thy loving prosper ever.
Heaven speed thee, poplar tree,
May thy wooing happy be.

GEN. Yet, the breeze is but a rover;
When he wings away,
Brook and poplar mourn a lover!
Sighing well-a-day!

ALL. Well-a-day!

GEN. Ah! the doing and undoing,
That the rogue could tell!

When the breeze is out a-wooing,
Who can woo so well?

POLICE. } Shocking tales the rogue could tell,
and } Nobody can woo so well.
PIRATES. } Pretty brook, thy dream is over,
For thy love is but a rover!
Sad the lot of poplar trees,
Courted by the fickle breeze!

[*Enter the* GENERAL'S *daughters, all in white peignoirs
and night-caps, and carrying lighted candles*

GIRLS. Now what is this, and what is that, and why does
father leave his rest
At such a time of night as this, so very incompletely
dressed?
Dear father is, and always was, the most methodical
of men!
It's his invariable rule to go to bed at half-past ten.
What strange occurrence can it be that calls dear
father from his rest
At such a time of night as this, so very incompletely
dressed?

Enter KING, SAMUEL, *and* FREDERIC

KING. Forward, my men, and seize that General there!
(*They seize the* GENERAL.)

GIRLS. The pirates! the pirates! Oh, despair!

PIRATES. Yes, we're the pirates, so despair!

GEN. Frederic here! Oh, joy! Oh, rapture!
Summon your men and effect their capture!

MABEL. Frederic, save us!

FRED. Beautiful Mabel,
I would if I could, but I am not able.

PIRATES. He's telling the truth, he is not able.

KING. With base deceit
You worked upon our feelings!
Revenge is sweet,
And flavours all our dealings!
With courage rare
And resolution manly,
For death prepare,
Unhappy General Stanley.

MABEL (*wildly*). Is he to die, unshriven—unannealed?

GIRLS. Oh, spare him!

MABEL. Will no one in his cause a weapon wield?

GIRLS. Oh, spare him!

POLICE (*springing up*). Yes, we are here, though hitherto
concealed!

GIRLS. Oh, rapture!

POLICE. So to the Constabulary, pirates, yield!

GIRLS. Oh, rapture!

[*A struggle ensues between Pirates and Police. Eventually the Police
are overcome, and fall prostrate, the Pirates standing over
them with drawn swords.*

Go, ye heroes, go to glory, . . .

CHORUS OF POLICE AND PIRATES

You ⎤
We ⎦ triumph now, for well we trow
    Our mortal career's cut short,
  No pirate band will take its stand
    At the Central Criminal Court.

SERG.   To gain a brief advantage you've contrived.
    But your proud triumph will not be long-lived.
KING.   Don't say you are orphans, for we know that game.
SERG.   On your allegiance we've a stronger claim—
    We charge you yield, in Queen Victoria's name!
KING (*baffled*). You do!
POLICE.   We do!
  We charge you yield, in Queen Victoria's name!

     [*Pirates kneel, Police stand over them triumphantly.*

KING. We yield at once, with humbled mien,
    Because, with all our faults, we love our Queen.
POLICE.   Yes, yes, with all their faults, they love their Queen.
GIRLS.   Yes, yes, with all, etc.

    [*Police, holding Pirates by the collar, take out
       handkerchiefs and weep.*

GEN.   Away with them, and place them at the bar!

       Enter RUTH

RUTH.   One moment! let me tell you who they are.
    They are no members of the common throng;
    They are all noblemen who have gone wrong!

GEN.   No Englishman unmoved that statement hears,
    Because, with all our faults, we love our House of
    Peers.

RECITATIVE—GENERAL

I pray you, pardon me, ex-Pirate King,
Peers will be peers, and youth will have its fling.
Resume your ranks and legislative duties,
And take my daughters, all of whom are beauties.

FINALE

Poor wandering ones!
    Though ye have surely strayed,
    Take heart of grace,
    Your steps retrace,
Poor wandering ones!

Poor wandering ones!
    If such poor love as ours
    Can help you find
    True peace of mind,
Why, take it, it is yours!
    Poor wandering ones! etc.

CURTAIN

THE MIKADO

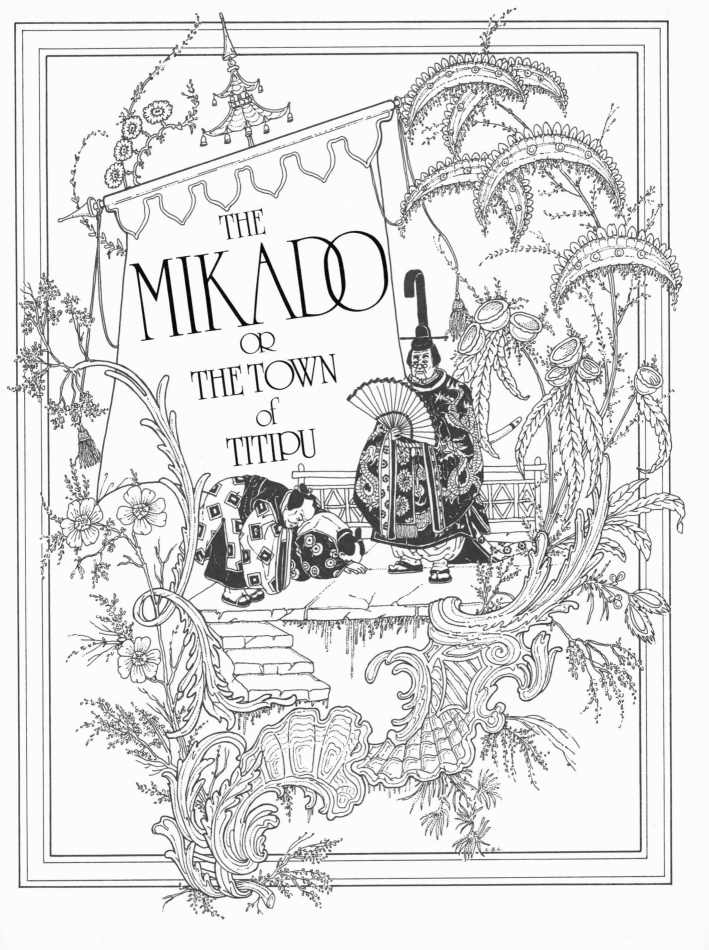

THE
MIKADO
OR
THE TOWN
of
TITIPU

DRAMATIS PERSONÆ

THE MIKADO OF JAPAN

NANKI-POO (*his Son, disguised as a wandering minstrel, and in love with* YUM-YUM)

KO-KO (*Lord High Executioner of Titipu*)

POOH-BAH (*Lord High Everything Else*)

PISH-TUSH (*a Noble Lord*)

YUM-YUM
PITTI-SING } *Three Sisters—Wards of* KO-KO
PEEP-BO

KATISHA (*an elderly Lady, in love with* NANKI-POO)

Chorus of School-girls, Nobles, Guards, and Coolies

ACT I

COURTYARD OF KO-KO'S OFFICIAL RESIDENCE

ACT II

KO-KO'S GARDEN

First produced at the Savoy Theatre on March 14, 1885

THE MIKADO
OR, THE TOWN of TITIPU

ACT I

SCENE.—*The courtyard of* KO-KO'S *Palace in Titipu. Japanese nobles discovered standing and sitting in attitudes suggested by native drawings.*

CHORUS OF NOBLES

If you want to know who we are,
    We are gentlemen of Japan;
On many a vase and jar—
    On many a screen and fan,
      We figure in lively paint:
      Our attitude's queer and quaint—
      You're wrong if you think it ain't, oh!

If you think we are worked by strings,
    Like a Japanese marionette,
You don't understand these things:
    It is simply Court etiquette.
      Perhaps you suppose this throng
      Can't keep it up all day long?
      If that's your idea, you're wrong, oh!

Enter NANKI-POO *in great excitement. He carries a native guitar on his back and a bundle of ballads in his hand.*

RECITATIVE—NANKI-POO

Gentlemen, I pray you tell me
Where a gentle maiden dwelleth,
Named Yum-Yum, the ward of Ko-Ko?
In pity speak—oh, speak, I pray you!

A NOBLE.   Why, who are you who ask this question?

NANK.   Come gather round me, and I'll tell you.

SONG AND CHORUS—NANKI-POO

A wandering minstrel I—
    A thing of shreds and patches,
    Of ballads, songs and snatches,
And dreamy lullaby!

My catalogue is long,

Through every passion ranging,
    And to your humours changing
I tune my supple song!

    Are you in sentimental mood?
      I'll sigh with you,
        Oh, sorrow, sorrow!
    On maiden's coldness do you brood?
      I'll do so, too—
        Oh, sorrow, sorrow!
    I'll charm your willing ears
    With songs of lovers' fears,
    While sympathetic tears
      My cheeks bedew—
        Oh, sorrow, sorrow!

But if patriotic sentiment is wanted,
    I've patriotic ballads cut and dried;
For where'er our country's banner may be planted,
    All other local banners are defied!
Our warriors, in serried ranks assembled,
    Never quail—or they conceal it if they do—
And I shouldn't be surprised if nations trembled
    Before the mighty troops of Titipu!

CHORUS.   We shouldn't be surprised, etc.

NANK.   And if you call for a song of the sea,
      We'll heave the capstan round,
    With a yeo heave ho, for the wind is free,
    Her anchor's a-trip and her helm's a-lee,
      Hurrah for the homeward bound!

CHORUS.   Yeo-ho—heave ho—
      Hurrah for the homeward bound!

NANK.   To lay aloft in a howling breeze
      May tickle a landsman's taste,
    But the happiest hour a sailor sees
      Is when he's down
      At an inland town,
    With his Nancy on his knees, yeo ho!
      And his arm around her waist!

CHORUS.
 Then man the capstan—off we go,
  As the fiddler swings us round,
   With a yeo heave ho,
   And a rumbelow,
   Hurrah for the homeward bound!

NANK. A wandering minstrel I, etc.

Enter PISH-TUSH

PISH. And what may be your business with Yum-Yum?

NANK. I'll tell you. A year ago I was a member of the Titipu town band. It was my duty to take the cap round for contributions. While discharging this delicate office, I saw Yum-Yum. We loved each other at once, but she was betrothed to her guardian Ko-Ko, a cheap tailor, and I saw that my suit was hopeless. Overwhelmed with despair, I quitted the town. Judge of my delight when I heard, a month ago, that Ko-Ko had been condemned to death for flirting! I hurried back at once, in the hope of finding Yum-Yum at liberty to listen to my protestations.

PISH. It is true that Ko-Ko was condemned to death for flirting, but he was reprieved at the last moment, and raised to the exalted rank of Lord High Executioner under the following remarkable circumstances:

SONG—PISH-TUSH *and* CHORUS

Our great Mikado, virtuous man,
When he to rule our land began,
  Resolved to try
  A plan whereby
Young men might best be steadied.
So he decreed, in words succinct,
That all who flirted, leered or winked
 (Unless connubially linked),
  Should forthwith be beheaded.

  And I expect you'll all agree
  That he was right to so decree.
   And I am right,
   And you are right,
   And all is right as right can be!

CHORUS.
   And you are right,
   And we are right, etc.

This stern decree, you'll understand,
Caused great dismay throughout the land!
  For young and old
  And shy and bold
  Were equally affected.
The youth who winked a roving eye,
Or breathed a non-connubial sigh,
Was thereupon condemned to die—
  He usually objected.

  And you'll allow, as I expect,
  That he was right to so object.

   And I am right,
   And you are right,
  And everything is quite correct!

CHORUS.
   And you are right,
   And we are right, etc.

And so we straight let out on bail,
A convict from the county jail,
  Whose head was next
  On some pretext
Condemnëd to be mown off,
And made *him* Headsman, for we said,
"Who's next to be decapited
Cannot cut off another's head
  Until he's cut his own off."

  And we are right, I think you'll say,
  To argue in this kind of way;
   And I am right,
   And you are right,
  And all is right—too-looral-lay!

CHORUS.
   And you are right,
   And we are right, etc.

[*Exeunt* CHORUS.

Enter POOH-BAH

NANK. Ko-Ko, the cheap tailor, Lord High Executioner of Titipu! Why, that's the highest rank a citizen can attain!

POOH. It is. Our logical Mikado, seeing no moral difference between the dignified judge who condemns a criminal to die, and the industrious mechanic who carries out the sentence, has rolled the two offices into one, and every judge is now his own executioner.

NANK. But how good of you (for I see that you are a nobleman of the highest rank) to condescend to tell all this to me, a mere strolling minstrel!

POOH. Don't mention it. I am, in point of fact, a particularly haughty and exclusive person, of pre-Adamite ancestral descent. You will understand this when I tell you that I can trace my ancestry back to a protoplasmal primordial atomic globule. Consequently, my family pride is something inconceivable. I can't help it. I was born sneering. But I struggle hard to overcome this defect. I mortify my pride continually. When all the great officers of State resigned in a body, because they were too proud to serve under an ex-tailor, did I not unhesitatingly accept all their posts at once?

PISH. And the salaries attached to them? You did.

POOH. It is consequently my degrading duty to serve this upstart as First Lord of the Treasury, Lord Chief Justice, Commander-in-Chief, Lord High Admiral, Master of the Buckhounds, Groom of the Back Stairs, Archbishop of Titipu, and Lord Mayor, both acting and elect, all rolled into one. And at a salary! A Pooh-Bah paid for his services! I a salaried minion! But I do it! It revolts me, but I do it!

A wandering minstel I—

NANK. And it does you credit.

POOH. But I don't stop at that. I go and dine with middle-class people on reasonable terms. I dance at cheap suburban parties for a moderate fee. I accept refreshment at any hands, however lowly. I also retail State secrets at a very low figure. For instance, any further information about Yum-Yum would come under the head of a State secret. (NANKI-POO *takes the hint, and gives him money.*) (*Aside.*) Another insult, and, I think, a light one!

SONG—POOH-BAH *with* NANKI-POO *and* PISH-TUSH

> Young man, despair,
>   Likewise go to,
> Yum-Yum the fair
>   You must not woo.
>   It will not do:
>   I'm sorry for you,
> You very imperfect ablutioner!
> This very day
>   From school Yum-Yum
> Will wend her way,
>   And homeward come,
>   With beat of drum
>   And a rum-tum-tum,
> To wed the Lord High Executioner!
> And the brass will crash,
>   And the trumpets bray,
>   And they'll cut a dash
>   On their wedding day.
> She'll toddle away, as all aver,
> With the Lord High Executioner!

NANK. *and* POOH. And the brass will crash, etc.

> It's a hopeless case,
>   As you may see,
> And in your place
>   Away I'd flee;
>   But don't blame me—
>   I'm sorry to be
> Of your pleasure a diminutioner.
>   They'll vow their pact
>   Extremely soon,
>   In point of fact
>   This afternoon.
>   Her honeymoon
>   With that buffoon
> At seven commences, so *you* shun her!

ALL.   And the brass will crash, etc.

[*Exit* PISH-TUSH.

RECITATIVE—NANKI-POO *and* POOH-BAH

NANK.   And I have journeyed for a month, or nearly,
    To learn that Yum-Yum, whom I love so dearly,
    This day to Ko-Ko is to be united!

POOH.   The fact appears to be as you've recited:
    But here he comes, equipped as suits his station;
    He'll give you any further information.
        [*Exeunt* POOH-BAH *and* NANKI-POO.

Enter CHORUS OF NOBLES

> Behold the Lord High Executioner
>   A personage of noble rank and title—
> A dignified and potent officer,
>   Whose functions are particularly vital!
>   Defer, defer,
>   To the Lord High Executioner!

Enter KO-KO *attended*

SOLO—KO-KO

> Taken from the county jail
>   By a set of curious chances;
> Liberated then on bail,
>   On my own recognizances;
> Wafted by a favouring gale
>   As one sometimes is in trances,
> To a height that few can scale,
>   Save by long and weary dances;
> Surely, never had a male
>   Under such like circumstances
> So adventurous a tale
>   Which may rank with most romances.

CHORUS.   Defer, defer,
        To the Lord High Executioner, etc.

KO. Gentlemen, I'm much touched by this reception. I can only trust that by strict attention to duty I shall ensure a continuance of those favours which it will ever be my study to deserve. If I should ever be called upon to act professionally, I am happy to think that there will be no difficulty in finding plenty of people whose loss will be a distinct gain to society at large.

SONG—KO-KO *with* CHORUS OF MEN

> As some day it may happen that a victim must be found,
>   I've got a little list—I've got a little list
> Of society offenders who might well be underground,
>   And who never would be missed—who never would be missed!
> There's the pestilential nuisances who write for autographs—
> All people who have flabby hands and irritating laughs—
> All children who are up in dates, and floor you with 'em flat—
> All persons who in shaking hands, shake hands with you like *that*—
> And all third persons who on spoiling *tête-à-têtes* insist—
>   They'd none of 'em be missed—they'd none of 'em be missed!

CHORUS. He's got 'em on the list—he's got 'em on the list;
        And they'll none of 'em be missed—they'll none of 'em be missed.

There's the banjo serenader, and the others of his race,
  And the piano-organist—I've got him on the list!
And the people who eat peppermint and puff it in your face,
  They never would be missed—they never would be missed!
Then the idiot who praises, with enthusiastic tone,
All centuries but this, and every country but his own;
And the lady from the provinces, who dresses like a guy,
And who "doesn't think she waltzes, but would rather like to
    try";
And that singular anomaly, the lady novelist—
  I don't think she'd be missed—I'm *sure* she'd not be missed!

CHORUS. He's got her on the list—he's got her on the list;
        And I don't think she'll be missed—I'm *sure* she'll
          not be missed!

And that *Nisi Prius* nuisance, who just now is rather rife,
  The Judicial humorist—I've got *him* on the list!
All funny fellows, comic men, and clowns of private life—
  They'd none of 'em be missed—they'd none of 'em be
    missed.
And apologetic statesmen of a compromising kind,
Such as—What d'ye call him—Thing'em-bob, and likewise—
    Never-mind,
And 'St—'st—'st—and What's-his-name, and also You-know-
    who—
The task of filling up the blanks I'd rather leave to *you*.
But it really doesn't matter whom you put upon the list,
  For they'd none of 'em be missed—they'd none of 'em be
    missed!

CHORUS. You may put 'em on the list—you may put 'em on
          the list;
        And they'll none of 'em be missed—they'll none
          of 'em be missed!

Enter POOH-BAH

KO. Pooh-bah, it seems that the festivities in connection
with my approaching marriage must last a week. I should like
to do it handsomely, and I want to consult you as to the
amount I ought to spend upon them.

POOH. Certainly. In which of my capacities? As First Lord
of the Treasury, Lord Chamberlain, Attorney-General, Chancellor of the Exchequer, Privy Purse, or Private Secretary?

KO. Suppose we say as Private Secretary.

POOH. Speaking as your Private Secretary, I should say that,
as the city will have to pay for it, don't stint yourself, do it
well.

KO. Exactly—as the city will have to pay for it. That is your
advice.

POOH. As Private Secretary. Of course you will understand
that, as Chancellor of the Exchequer, I am bound to see that
due economy is observed.

KO. Oh! But you said just now "Don't stint yourself, do it
well."

POOH. As Private Secretary.

KO. And now you say that due economy must be observed.

POOH. As Chancellor of the Exchequer.

KO. I see. Come over here, where the Chancellor can't hear
us. (*They cross the stage.*) Now, as my Solicitor, how do you
advise me to deal with this difficulty?

POOH. Oh, as your Solicitor, I should have no hesitation in
saying "Chance it—"

KO. Thank you. (*Shaking his hand.*) I will.

POOH. If it were not that, as Lord Chief Justice, I am
bound to see that the law isn't violated.

KO. I see. Come over here where the Chief Justice can't
hear us. (*They cross the stage.*) Now, then, as First Lord of the
Treasury?

POOH. Of course, as First Lord of the Treasury, I could
propose a special vote that would cover all expenses, if it were
not that, as Leader of the Opposition, it would be my duty to
resist it, tooth and nail. Or, as Paymaster-General, I could so
cook the accounts that, as Lord High Auditor, I should never
discover the fraud. But then, as Archbishop of Titipu, it
would be my duty to denounce my dishonesty and give myself into my own custody as First Commissioner of Police.

KO. That's extremely awkward.

POOH. I don't say that all these distinguished people
couldn't be squared; but it is right to tell you that they
wouldn't be sufficiently degraded in their own estimation unless they were insulted with a very considerable bribe.

KO. The matter shall have my careful consideration. But
my bride and her sisters approach, and any little compliment
on your part, such as an abject grovel in a characteristic Japanese attitude, would be esteemed a favour.

                                        [*Exeunt together.*

Enter procession of YUM-YUM'S *schoolfellows, heralding*
YUM-YUM, PEEP-BO, *and* PITTI-SING

CHORUS OF GIRLS

Comes a train of little ladies
  From scholastic trammels free,
Each a little bit afraid is,
  Wondering what the world can be!

Is it but a world of trouble—
  Sadness set to song?
Is its beauty but a bubble
  Bound to break ere long?

Are its palaces and pleasures
  Fantasies that fade?
And the glory of its treasures
  Shadow of a shade?

Schoolgirls we, eighteen and under,
  From scholastic trammels free,
And we wonder—how we wonder!—
  What on earth the world can be!

TRIO

YUM-YUM, PEEP-BO, *and* PITTI-SING, *with* CHORUS OF GIRLS

THE THREE.	Three little maids from school are we,
	Pert as a school-girl well can be,
	Filled to the brim with girlish glee,
	Three little maids from school!
YUM-YUM.	Everything is a source of fun. (*Chuckle.*)
PEEP-BO.	Nobody's safe, for we care for none!
	(*Chuckle.*)
PITTI-SING.	Life is a joke that's just begun! (*Chuckle.*)
THE THREE.	Three little maids from school!
ALL (*dancing*)	Three little maids who, all unwary,
	Come from a ladies' seminary,
	Freed from its genius tutelary—
THE THREE (*suddenly demure*).	Three little maids from school!

YUM-YUM.	One little maid is a bride, Yum-Yum—
PEEP-BO.	Two little maids in attendance come—
PITTI-SING.	Three little maids is the total sum.
THE THREE.	Three little maids from school!
YUM-YUM.	From three little maids take one away.
PEEP-BO.	Two little maids remain, and they—
PITTI-SING.	Won't have to wait very long, they say—
THE THREE.	Three little maids from school!
ALL (*dancing*).	Three little maids who, all unwary,
	Come from a ladies' seminary,
	Freed from its genius tutelary—
THE THREE (*suddenly demure*).	Three little maids from school!

Enter KO-KO *and* POOH-BAH

KO. At last, my bride that is to be! (*About to embrace her.*)

YUM. You're not going to kiss me before all these people?

KO. Well, that was the idea.

YUM. (*aside to* PEEP-BO). It seems odd, doesn't it?

PEEP. It's rather peculiar.

PITTI. Oh, I expect it's all right. Must have a beginning, you know.

YUM. Well, of course I know nothing about these things; but I've no objection if it's usual.

KO. Oh, it's quite usual, I think. Eh, Lord Chamberlain? (*Appealing to* POOH-BAH.)

POOH. I have known it done. (KO-KO *embraces her.*)

YUM. Thank goodness that's over! (*Sees* NANKI-POO, *and rushes to him.*) Why, that's never you? (*The Three Girls rush to him and shake his hands, all speaking at once.*)

YUM. Oh, I'm so glad! I haven't seen you for ever so long, and I'm right at the top of the school, and I've got three prizes, and I've come home for good, and I'm not going back any more!

PEEP. And have you got an engagement?—Yum-Yum's got one, but she doesn't like it, and she'd ever so much rather it was you! I've come home for good, and I'm not going back any more!

PITTI. Now tell us all the news, because you go about everywhere, and we've been at school, but, thank goodness, that's all over now, and we've come home for good, and we're not going back any more!

(*These three speeches are spoken together in one breath.*)

KO. I beg your pardon. Will you present me?

YUM. Oh, this is the musician who used—

PEEP. Oh, this is the gentleman who used—

PITTI. Oh, it is only Nanki-Poo who used—

KO. One at a time, if you please.

YUM. Oh, if you please, he's the gentleman who used to play so beautifully on the—on the—

PITTI. On the Marine Parade.

YUM. Yes, I think that was the name of the instrument.

NANK. Sir, I have the misfortune to love your ward, Yum-Yum—oh, I know I deserve your anger!

KO. Anger! not a bit, my boy. Why, I love her myself. Charming little girl, isn't she? Pretty eyes, nice hair. Taking little thing, altogether. Very glad to hear my opinion backed by a competent authority. Thank you very much. Good-bye. (*To* PISH-TUSH.) Take him away. (PISH-TUSH *removes him.*)

PITTI (*who has been examining* POOH-BAH). I beg your pardon, but what is this? Customer come to try on?

KO. That is a Tremendous Swell.

PITTI. Oh, it's alive. (*She starts back in alarm.*)

POOH. Go away, little girls. Can't talk to little girls like you. Go away, there's dears.

KO. Allow me to present you, Pooh-Bah. These are my three wards. The one in the middle is my bride elect.

POOH. What do you want me to do to them? Mind, I *will not* kiss them.

KO. No, no, you shan't kiss them; a little bow—a mere nothing—you needn't mean it, you know.

POOH. It goes against my grain. They are not young ladies, they are young persons.

KO. Come, come, make an effort, there's a good nobleman.

POOH. (*aside to* KO-KO). Well, I shan't mean it. (*With a great effort.*) How de do, little girls, how de do? (*Aside.*) Oh, my protoplasmal ancestor!

KO. That's very good. (*Girls indulge in suppressed laughter.*)

POOH. I see nothing to laugh at. It is very painful to me to have to say "How de do, little girls, how de do?" to young persons. I'm not in the habit of saying "How de do, little girls, how de do?" to anybody under the rank of a Stockbroker.

KO. (*aside to girls*). Don't laugh at him, he can't help it—he's under treatment for it. (*Aside to* POOH-BAH.) Never mind them, they don't understand the delicacy of your position.

POOH. We know how delicate it is, don't we?

KO. I should think we did! How a nobleman of your importance can do it at all is a thing I never can, never shall understand.

[KO-KO *retires up and goes off.*

QUARTETTE AND CHORUS OF GIRLS
YUM-YUM, PEEP-BO, PITTI-SING, *and* POOH-BAH

YUM., PEEP.	So please you, Sir, we much regret
and PITTI.	If we have failed in etiquette

Three little maids from school are we, . . .

Towards a man of rank so high—
We shall know better by and by.

YUM. But youth, of course, must have its fling,
So pardon us,
So pardon us,

PITTI. And don't, in girlhood's happy spring,
Be hard on us,
Be hard on us,
If we're inclined to dance and sing.
Tra la la, etc. (*Dancing.*)

CHORUS OF GIRLS. But youth, of course, etc.

POOH. I think you ought to recollect
You cannot show too much respect
Towards the highly titled few;
But nobody does, and why should you?
That youth at us should have its fling,
Is hard on us,
Is hard on us;
To our prerogative we cling—
So pardon us,
So pardon us,
If we decline to dance and sing.
Tra la la, etc. (*Dancing.*)

CHORUS OF GIRLS. But youth, of course, must have its fling,
etc.

[*Exeunt all but* YUM-YUM.

Enter NANKI-POO

NANK. Yum-Yum, at last we are alone! I have sought you night and day for three weeks, in the belief that your guardian was beheaded, and I find that you are about to be married to him this afternoon!

YUM. Alas, yes!

NANK. But you do not love him?

YUM. Alas, no!

NANK. Modified rapture! But why do you not refuse him?

YUM. What good would that do? He's my guardian, and he wouldn't let me marry you!

NANK. But I would wait until you were of age!

YUM. You forget that in Japan girls do not arrive at years of discretion until they are fifty.

NANK. True; from seventeen to forty-nine are considered years of indiscretion.

YUM. Besides—a wandering minstel, who plays a wind instrument outside tea-houses, is hardly a fitting husband for the ward of a Lord High Executioner.

NANK. But— (*Aside.*) Shall I tell her? Yes! She will not betray me! (*Aloud.*) What if it should prove that, after all, I am no musician?

YUM. There! I was certain of it, directly I heard you play!

NANK. What if it should prove that I am no other than the son of his Majesty the Mikado?

YUM. The son of the Mikado! But why is your Highness disguised? And what has your Highness done? And will your Highness promise never to do it again?

NANK. Some years ago I had the misfortune to captivate Katisha, an elderly lady of my father's Court. She misconstrued my customary affability into expressions of affection, and claimed me in marriage, under my father's law. My father, the Lucius Junius Brutus of his race, ordered me to marry her within a week, or perish ignominiously on the scaffold. That night I fled his Court, and, assuming the disguise of a Second Trombone, I joined the band in which you found me when I had the happiness of seeing you! (*Approaching her.*)

YUM. (*retreating*). If you please, I think your Highness had better not come too near. The laws against flirting are excessively severe.

NANK. But we are quite alone, and nobody can see us.

YUM. Still, that doesn't make it right. To flirt is capital.

NANK. It *is* capital!

YUM. And we must obey the law.

NANK. Deuce take the law!

YUM. I wish it would, but it won't!

NANK. If it were not for that, how happy we might be!

YUM. Happy indeed!

NANK. If it were not for the law, we should now be sitting side by side, like that. (*Sits by her.*)

YUM. Instead of being obliged to sit half a mile off, like that. (*Crosses and sits at other side of stage.*)

NANK. We should be gazing into each other's eyes, like that. (*Gazing at her sentimentally.*)

YUM. Breathing sighs of unutterable love—like that. (*Sighing and gazing lovingly at him.*)

NANK. With our arms round each other's waists, like that. (*Embracing her.*)

YUM. Yes, if it wasn't for the law.

NANK. If it wasn't for the law.

YUM. As it is, of course we couldn't do anything of the kind.

NANK. Not for worlds!

YUM. Being engaged to Ko-Ko, you know!

NANK. Being engaged to Ko-Ko!

DUET—YUM-YUM *and* NANKI-POO

NANK. Were you not to Ko-Ko plighted,
I would say in tender tone,
"Loved one, let us be united—
Let us be each other's own!"
I would merge all rank and station,
Worldly sneers are nought to us,
And, to mark my admiration,
I would kiss you fondly thus—

(*Kisses her.*)

BOTH. I | would kiss | you | fondly thus— (*Kiss.*)
He | | me |

YUM. But as I'm engaged to Ko-Ko,
To embrace you thus, *con fuoco*,
Would be distinctly no *giuoco*,
And for yam I should get toko—

BOTH.   Toko, toko, toko, toko!

NANK.   So, in spite of all temptation,
　　　　　　Such a theme I'll not discuss,
　　　　　　And on no consideration
　　　　　　Will I kiss you fondly thus—

　　　　　　　　　　　　　　　　　　(*Kissing her.*)

　　　　　　Let me make it clear to you,
　　　　　　This is what I'll never do!
　　　　　　This, oh, this, oh, this, oh, this—

　　　　　　　　　　　　　　　　　　(*Kissing her.*)

TOGETHER.   This, oh, this, etc.

　　　　　　　　　　　[Exeunt in opposite directions.

Enter KO-KO

KO. (*looking after* YUM-YUM). There she goes! To think how entirely my future happiness is wrapped up in that little parcel! Really, it hardly seems worth while! Oh, matrimony!— (*Enter* POOH-BAH *and* PISH-TUSH.) Now then, what is it? Can't you see I'm soliloquizing? You have interrupted an apostrophe, sir!

PISH. I am the bearer of a letter from his Majesty the Mikado.

KO. (*taking it from him reverentially*). A letter from the Mikado! What in the world can he have to say to me? (*Reads letter.*) Ah, here it is at last! I thought it would come sooner or later! The Mikado is struck by the fact that no executions have taken place in Titipu for a year and decrees that unless somebody is beheaded within one month the post of Lord High Executioner shall be abolished, and the city reduced to the rank of a village!

PISH. But that will involve us all in irretrievable ruin!

KO. Yes. There is no help for it, I shall have to execute somebody at once. The only question is, who shall it be?

POOH. Well, it seems unkind to say so, but as you're already under sentence of death for flirting, everything seems to point to *you.*

KO. To me? What are you talking about? I can't execute myself.

POOH. Why not?

KO. Why not? Because, in the first place, self-decapitation is an extremely difficult, not to say dangerous, thing to attempt; and, in the second, it's suicide, and suicide is a capital offence.

POOH. That is so, no doubt.

PISH. We might reserve that point.

POOH. True, it could be argued six months hence, before the full Court.

KO. Besides, I don't see how a man *can* cut off his own head.

POOH. A man might try.

PISH. Even if you only succeeded in cutting it half off, that would be something.

POOH. It would be taken as an earnest of your desire to comply with the Imperial will.

KO. No. Pardon me, but there I am adamant. As official Headsman, my reputation is at stake, and I can't consent to embark on a professional operation unless I see my way to a successful result.

POOH. This professional conscientiousness is highly creditable to *you,* but it places us in a very awkward position.

KO. My good sir, the awkwardness of your position is grace itself compared with that of a man engaged in the act of cutting off his own head.

PISH. I am afraid that, unless you can obtain a substitute—

KO. A substitute? Oh, certainly—nothing easier. (*To* POOH-BAH.) I appoint you Lord High Substitute.

POOH. I should be delighted. Such an appointment would realize my fondest dreams. But no, at any sacrifice, I must set bounds to my insatiable ambition!

TRIO

KO-KO	POOH-BAH	PISH-TUSH
My brain it teems	I am so proud,	I heard one day
With endless schemes	If I allowed	A gentleman say
Both good and new	My family pride	That criminals who
For Titipu;	To be my guide,	Are cut in two
But if I flit,	I'd volunteer	Can hardly feel
The benefit	To quit this sphere	The fatal steel,
That I'd diffuse	Instead of you,	And so are slain
The town would lose!	In a minute or two.	Without much pain.
Now every man	But family pride	If this is true,
To aid his clan	Must be denied,	It's jolly for you;
Should plot and plan	And set aside,	Your courage screw
As best he can,	And mortified.	To bid us adieu,
And so,	And so,	And go
Although	Although	And show
I'm ready to go,	I wish to go,	Both friend and foe
Yet recollect	And greatly pine	How much you dare.
'Twere disrespect	To brightly shine,	I'm quite aware
Did I neglect	And take the line	It's your affair,
To thus effect	Of a hero fine,	Yet I declare
This aim direct,	With grief condign	I'd take your share,
So I object—	I must decline—	But I don't much care—
So I object—	I must decline—	I don't much care—
So I object—	I must decline—	I don't much care—

ALL.   To sit in solemn silence in a dull, dark dock,
　　　　　　In a pestilential prison, with a life-long lock,
　　　　　　Awaiting the sensation of a short, sharp shock,
　　　　　　From a cheap and chippy chopper on a big black block!

　　　　　　　　　　　[Exeunt POOH. *and* PISH.

KO. This is simply appalling! I, who allowed myself to be respited at the last moment, simply in order to benefit my native town, am now required to die within a month, and that by a man whom I have loaded with honours! Is this public gratitude? Is this— (*Enter* NANKI-POO, *with a rope in his hands.*) Go away, sir! How dare you? Am I never to be permitted to soliloquize?

NANK. Oh, go on—don't mind me.

KO. What are you going to do with that rope?

NANK. I am about to terminate an unendurable existence.

KO. Terminate your existence? Oh, nonsense! What for?

NANK. Because you are going to marry the girl I adore.

KO. Nonsense, sir. I won't permit it. I am a humane man, and if you attempt anything of the kind I shall order your instant arrest. Come, sir, desist at once or I summon my guard.

NANK. That's absurd. If you attempt to raise an alarm, I instantly perform the Happy Despatch with this dagger.

KO. No, no, don't do that. This is horrible! (*Suddenly.*) Why, you cold-blooded scoundrel, are you aware that, in taking your life, you are committing a crime which–which–which is– Oh! (*Struck by an idea.*) Substitute!

NANK. What's the matter?

KO. Is it *absolutely certain* that you are resolved to die?

NANK. Absolutely!

KO. Will *nothing* shake your resolution?

NANK. Nothing.

KO. Threats, entreaties, prayers–all useless?

NANK. All! My mind is made up.

KO. Then, if you really mean what you say, and if you are absolutely resolved to die, and if nothing whatever will shake your determination–don't spoil yourself by committing suicide, but be beheaded handsomely at the hands of the Public Executioner!

NANK. I don't see how that would benefit me.

KO. You don't? Observe: you'll have a month to live, and you'll live like a fighting-cock at my expense. When the day comes there'll be a grand public ceremonial–you'll be the central figure–no one will attempt to deprive you of that distinction. There'll be a procession–bands–dead march–bells tolling–all the girls in tears–Yum-Yum distracted–then, when it's all over, general rejoicings, and a display of fireworks in the evening. *You* won't see them, but they'll be there all the same.

NANK. Do you think Yum-Yum would really be distracted at my death?

KO. I am convinced of it. Bless you, she's the most tender-hearted little creature alive.

NANK. I should be sorry to cause her pain. Perhaps, after all, if I were to withdraw from Japan, and travel in Europe for a couple of years, I might contrive to forget her.

KO. Oh, I don't think you could forget Yum-Yum so easily; and, after all, what is more miserable than a love-blighted life?

NANK. True.

KO. Life without Yum-Yum–why, it seems absurd!

NANK. And yet there are a good many people in the world who have to endure it.

KO. Poor devils, yes! You are quite right not to be of their number.

NANK. (*suddenly*). I *won't* be of their number!

KO. Noble fellow!

NANK. I'll tell you how we'll manage it. Let me marry Yum-Yum to-morrow, and in a month you may behead me.

KO. No, no. I draw the line at Yum-Yum.

NANK. Very good. If you can draw the line, so can I. (*Preparing rope.*)

KO. Stop, stop–listen one moment–be reasonable. How can I consent to your marrying Yum-Yum if I'm going to marry her myself?

NANK. My good friend, she'll be a widow in a month, and you can marry her then.

KO. That's true, of course. I quite see that. But, dear me! my position during the next month will be most unpleasant–most unpleasant.

NANK. Not half so unpleasant as my position at the end of it.

KO. But–dear me!–well–I agree–after all, it's only putting off my wedding for a month. But you won't prejudice her against me, will you? You see, I've educated her to be my wife; she's been taught to regard me as a wise and good man. Now I shouldn't like her views on that point disturbed.

NANK. Trust me, she shall never learn the truth from me.

FINALE

Enter CHORUS, POOH-BAH, *and* PISH-TUSH

CHORUS

> With aspect stern
>   And gloomy stride,
> We come to learn
>   How you decide.
>
> Don't hesitate
>   Your choice to name,
> A dreadful fate
>   You'll suffer all the same.

POOH. To ask you what you mean to do we punctually appear.

KO. Congratulate me, gentlemen, I've found a Volunteer!

ALL. The Japanese equivalent for Hear, Hear, Hear!

KO. (*presenting him*).   'Tis Nanki-Poo!

ALL.   Hail, Nanki-Poo!

KO.   I think he'll do?

ALL.   Yes, yes, he'll do!

KO. He yields his life if I'll Yum-Yum surrender.
Now I adore that girl with passion tender,
And could not yield her with a ready will,
        Or her allot
        If I did not
Adore myself with passion tenderer still!

Enter YUM-YUM, PEEP-BO, *and* PITTI-SING

ALL.   Ah, yes!
He loves himself with passion tenderer still!

KO. (*to* NANKI-POO). Take her–she's yours!

[*Exit* KO-KO.

ENSEMBLE

NANKI-POO. The threatened cloud has passed away,
YUM-YUM. And brightly shines the dawning day;
NANKI-POO. What though the night may come too soon,
YUM-YUM. There's yet a month of afternoon!

NANKI-POO, POOH-BAH, YUM-YUM, PITTI-SING,
and PEEP-BO

Then let the throng
Our joy advance,
With laughing song
And merry dance,

CHORUS. With joyous shout and ringing cheer,
Inaugurate our brief career!

PITTI-SING. A day, a week, a month, a year—
YUM. Or far or near, or far or near,
POOH. Life's eventime comes much too soon,
PITTI-SING. You'll live at least a honeymoon!

ALL. Then let the throng, etc.

CHORUS. With joyous shout, etc.

SOLO—POOH-BAH

As in a month you've got to die,
If Ko-Ko tells us true,
'Twere empty compliment to cry
"Long life to Nanki-Poo!"
But as one month you have to live
As fellow-citizen,
This toast with three times three we'll give—
"Long life to you—till then!"

[*Exit* POOH-BAH.

CHORUS. May all good fortune prosper you,
May you have health and riches too,
May you succeed in all you do!
Long life to you—till then!

(*Dance.*)

Enter KATISHA *melodramatically*

KAT. Your revels cease! Assist me, all of you!
CHORUS. Why, who is this whose evil eyes
Rain blight on our festivities?
KAT. I claim my perjured lover, Nanki-Poo!
Oh, fool! to shun delights that never cloy!
CHORUS. Go, leave thy deadly work undone!
KAT. Come back, oh, shallow fool! come back to joy!
CHORUS. Away, away! ill-favoured one!
NANK. (*aside to* YUM-YUM). Ah!
'Tis Katisha!
The maid of whom I told you. (*About to go.*)

KAT. (*detaining him*). No!
You shall not go,
These arms shall thus enfold you!

SONG—KATISHA

KAT. (*addressing* NANKI-POO).
Oh fool, that fleest
My hallowed joys!
Oh blind, that seest
No equipoise!
Oh rash, that judgest
From half, the whole!
Oh base, that grudgest
Love's lightest dole!
Thy heart unbind,
Oh fool, oh blind!
Give me my place,
Oh rash, oh base!

CHORUS. If she's thy bride, restore her place,
Oh fool, oh blind, oh rash, oh base!

KAT. (*addressing* YUM-YUM).
Pink cheek, that rulest
Where wisdom serves!
Bright eye, that foolest
Heroic nerves!
Rose lip, that scornest
Lore-laden years!
Smooth tongue, that warnest
Who rightly hears!
Thy doom is nigh,
Pink cheek, bright eye!
Thy knell is rung,
Rose lip, smooth tongue!

CHORUS. If true her tale, thy knell is rung,
Pink cheek, bright eye, rose lip, smooth tongue!

PITTI-SING. Away, nor prosecute your quest—
From our intention, well expressed,
You cannot turn us!
The state of your connubial views
Towards the person you accuse
Does not concern us!
For he's going to marry Yum-Yum—
ALL. Yum-Yum!
PITTI. Your anger pray bury,
For all will be merry,
I think you had better succumb—
AL. Cumb—cumb!
PITTI. And join our expressions of glee.
On this subject I pray you be dumb—
ALL. Dumb—dumb.
PITTI. You'll find there are many
Who'll wed for a penny—
The word for your guidance is "Mum"—
ALL. Mum—mum!
PITTI. There's lots of good fish in the sea!

ALL. On this subject we pray you be dumb, etc.

SOLO—KATISHA

The hour of gladness
    Is dead and gone;
In silent sadness
    I live alone!
The hope I cherished
    All lifeless lies,
And all has perished
    Save love, which never dies!
Oh, faithless one, this insult you shall rue!
In vain for mercy on your knees you'll sue.
    I'll tear the mask from your disguising!

NANK. (*aside*).   Now comes the blow!
KAT.   Prepare yourselves for news surprising!
NANK. (*aside*).   How foil my foe?
KAT.   No minstrel he, despite bravado!
YUM. (*aside, struck by an idea*).   Ha! ha! I know!
KAT.   He is the son of your—

[NANKI-POO, YUM-YUM, *and* CHORUS, *interrupting, sing Japanese words, to drown her voice.*

ALL.   O ni! bikkuri shakkuri to!
KAT.   In vain you interrupt with this tornado!
    He is the only son of your—
ALL.   O ni! bikkuri shakkuri to!
KAT.   I'll spoil—
ALL.   O ni! bikkuri shakkuri to!
KAT.   Your gay gambado!
    He is the son—
ALL.   O ni! bikkuri shakkuri to!
KAT.   Of your—
ALL.   O ni! bikkuri shakkuri to!
KAT.   The son of your—
ALL.   O ni! bikkuri shakkuri to! oya! oya!

ENSEMBLE

KATISHA	THE OTHERS
Ye torrents roar!	We'll hear no more,
Ye tempests howl!	Ill-omened owl,
Your wrath outpour	To joy we soar,
With angry growl!	Despite your scowl!
Do ye your worst, my vengeance call	The echoes of our festival
Shall rise triumphant over all!	Shall rise triumphant over all!
Prepare for woe,	Away you go,
Ye haughty lords,	Collect your hordes;
At once I go	Proclaim your woe
Mikado-wards,	In dismal chords;
My wrongs with vengeance shall be crowned!	We do not heed their dismal sound,
My wrongs with vengeance shall be crowned!	For joy reigns everywhere around.

[KATISHA *rushes furiously up stage, clearing the crowd away right and left, finishing on steps at the back of stage.*

END OF ACT I

ACT II

SCENE.—KO-KO'S *Garden*

YUM-YUM *discovered seated at her bridal toilet, surrounded by maidens, who are dressing her hair and painting her face and lips, as she judges of the effect in a mirror.*

SOLO—PITTI-SING *and* CHORUS OF GIRLS

CHORUS.   Braid the raven hair—
    Weave the supple tress—
    Deck the maiden fair,
      In her loveliness—
    Paint the pretty face—
    Dye the coral lip—
    Emphasize the grace
      Of her ladyship!
    Art and nature, thus allied,
    Go to make a pretty bride.

SOLO—PITTI-SING

Sit with downcast eye—
    Let it brim with dew—
Try if you can cry—
    We will do so, too.
When you're summoned, start
    Like a frightened doe—
Flutter, little heart,
    Colour, come and go!
Modesty at marriage-tide
Well becomes a pretty bride!

CHORUS

Braid the raven hair, etc.

[*Exeunt* PITTI-SING, PEEP-BO, *and* CHORUS.

YUM. Yes, I am indeed beautiful! Sometimes I sit and wonder, in my artless Japanese way, why it is that I am so much more attractive than anybody else in the whole world. Can this be vanity? No! Nature is lovely and rejoices in her loveliness. I am a child of Nature, and take after my mother.

SONG—YUM-YUM

The sun, whose rays
Are all ablaze
    With ever-living glory,
Does not deny
His majesty—
    He scorns to tell a story!
He don't exclaim,
"I blush for shame,
    So kindly be indulgent."
But, fierce and bold,
In fiery gold,
    He glorifies all effulgent!

A more humane Mikado never / Did in Japan exist, . . .

I mean to rule the earth,
  As he the sky—
We really know our worth,
  The sun and I!

Observe his flame,
That placid dame,
  The moon's Celestial Highness;
There's not a trace
Upon her face
  Of diffidence or shyness:
She borrows light
That, through the night,
  Mankind may all acclaim her!
And, truth to tell,
She lights up well,
  So I, for one, don't blame her!

  Ah, pray make no mistake,
    We are not shy;
  We're very wide awake,
    The moon and I!

Enter PITTI-SING *and* PEEP-BO

YUM. Yes, everything seems to smile upon me. I am to be married to-day to the man I love best, and I believe I am the very happiest girl in Japan!

PEEP. The happiest girl indeed, for she is indeed to be envied who has attained happiness in all but perfection.

YUM. In "all but" perfection?

PEEP. Well, dear, it can't be denied that the fact that your husband is to be beheaded in a month is, in its way, a drawback. It does seem to take the top off it, you know.

PITTI. I don't know about that. It all depends!

PEEP. At all events, *he* will find it a drawback.

PITTI. Not necessarily. Bless you, it all depends!

YUM. (*in tears*). I think it very indelicate of you to refer to such a subject on such a day. If my married happiness *is* to be—to be—

PEEP. Cut short.

YUM. Well, cut short—in a month, can't you let me forget it? (*Weeping.*)

Enter NANKI-POO, *followed by* PISH-TUSH

NANK. Yum-Yum in tears—and on her wedding morn!

YUM. (*sobbing*). They've been reminding me that in a month you're to be beheaded! (*Bursts into tears.*)

PITTI. Yes, we've been reminding her that you're to be beheaded. (*Bursts into tears.*)

PEEP. It's quite true, you know, you *are* to be beheaded! (*Bursts into tears.*)

NANK. (*aside*). Humph! Now, some bridegrooms would be depressed by this sort of thing! (*Aloud.*) A month? Well, what's a month? Bah! These divisions of time are purely arbitrary. Who says twenty-four hours make a day?

PITTI. There's a popular impression to that effect.

NANK. Then we'll efface it. We'll call each second a minute—each minute an hour—each hour a day—and each day a year. At that rate we've about thirty years of married happiness before us!

PEEP. And, at that rate, this interview has already lasted four hours and three-quarters!

[*Exit* PEEP-BO.

YUM. (*still sobbing*). Yes. How time flies when one is thoroughly enjoying oneself.

NANK. That's the way to look at it! Don't let's be downhearted! There's a silver lining to every cloud.

YUM. Certainly. Let's—let's be perfectly happy! (*Almost in tears.*)

PISH-TUSH. By all means. Let's—let's thoroughly enjoy ourselves.

PITTI. It's—it's absurd to cry. (*Trying to force a laugh.*)

YUM. Quite ridiculous! (*Trying to laugh.*)

[*All break into a forced and melancholy laugh.*

MADRIGAL
YUM-YUM, PITTI-SING, NANKI-POO, *and* PISH-TUSH

Brightly dawns our wedding day;
  Joyous hour, we give thee greeting!
  Whither, whither art thou fleeting?
Fickle moment, prithee stay!
  What though mortal joys be hollow?
  Pleasures come, if sorrows follow:
Though the tocsin sound, ere long,
  Ding dong! Ding dong!
Yet until the shadows fall
Over one and over all,
Sing a merry madrigal—
    A madrigal!

Fal-la—fal-la! etc. (*Ending in tears.*)

Let us dry the ready tear,
  Though the hours are surely creeping
  Little need for woeful weeping,
Till the sad sundown is near.
  All must sip the cup of sorrow—
  I to-day and thou to-morrow;
This the close of every song—
  Ding dong! Ding dong!
What, though solemn shadows fall,
Sooner, later, over all?
Sing a merry madrigal—
    A madrigal!

Fal-la—fal-la! etc. (*Ending in tears.*)

[*Exeunt* PITTI-SING *and* PISH-TUSH.

[NANKI-POO *embraces* YUM-YUM. *Enter* KO-KO.
NANKI-POO *releases* YUM-YUM.

72

KO. Go on—don't mind me.

NANK. I'm afraid we're distressing you.

KO. Never mind, I must get used to it. Only please do it by degrees. Begin by putting your arm round her waist. (NANKI-POO *does so.*) There; let me get used to that first.

YUM. Oh, wouldn't you like to retire? It must pain you to see us so affectionate together!

KO. No, I must learn to bear it! Now oblige me by allowing her head to rest on your shoulder.

NANK. Like that? (*He does so.* KO-KO *much affected.*)

KO. I am much obliged to you. Now—kiss her! (*He does so.* KO-KO *writhes with anguish.*) Thank you—it's simple torture!

YUM. Come, come, bear up. After all, it's only for a month.

KO. No. It's no use deluding oneself with false hopes.

NANK. ⎫
YUM. ⎬ What do you mean?

KO. (*to* YUM-YUM). My child—my poor child! (*Aside.*) How shall I break it to her? (*Aloud.*) My little bride that was to have been?

YUM. (*delighted*). *Was* to have been?

KO. Yes, you never can be mine!

NANK. ⎫ (*in ecstasy.*) What!
YUM. ⎬ I'm so glad!

KO. I've just ascertained that, by the Mikado's law, when a married man is beheaded his wife is buried alive.

NANK. ⎫
YUM. ⎬ Buried alive!

KO. Buried alive. It's a most unpleasant death.

NANK. But whom did you get that from?

KO. Oh, from Pooh-Bah. He's my Solicitor.

YUM. But he may be mistaken!

KO. So I thought; so I consulted the Attorney-General, the Lord Chief Justice, the Master of the Rolls, the Judge Ordinary, and the Lord Chancellor. They're all of the same opinion. Never knew such unanimity on a point of law in my life!

NANK. But stop a bit! This law has never been put in force.

KO. Not yet. You see, flirting is the only crime punishable with decapitation, and married men never flirt.

NANK. Of course, they don't. I quite forgot that! Well, I suppose I may take it that my dream of happiness is at an end!

YUM. Darling—I don't want to appear selfish, and I love you with all my heart—I don't suppose I shall ever love anybody else half as much—but when I agreed to marry you—my own—I had no idea—pet—that I should have to be buried alive in a month!

NANK. Nor I! It's the very first I've heard of it!

YUM. It—it makes a difference, doesn't it?

NANK. It *does* make a difference, of course.

YUM. You see—burial alive—it's such a stuffy death!

NANK. I call it a beast of a death.

YUM. You see my difficulty, don't you?

NANK. Yes, and I see my own. If I insist on your carrying out your promise, I doom you to a hideous death; if I release you, you marry Ko-Ko at once!

TRIO—YUM-YUM, NANKI-POO, *and* KO-KO

YUM.   Here's a how-de-do!
                 If I marry you,
        When your time has come to perish,
        Then the maiden whom you cherish
                 Must be slaughtered, too!
                 Here's a how-de-do!

NANK.   Here's a pretty mess!
                 In a month, or less,
        I must die without a wedding!
        Let the bitter tears I'm shedding
                 Witness my distress,
                 Here's a pretty mess!

KO.   Here's a state of things!
                 To her life she clings!
        Matrimonial devotion
        Doesn't seem to suit her notion—
                 Burial it brings!
                 Here's a state of things!

ENSEMBLE

YUM-YUM *and* NANKI-POO	KO-KO
With a passion that's intense	With a passion that's intense
I worship and adore,	You worship and adore,
But the laws of common sense	But the laws of common sense
We oughtn't to ignore.	You oughtn't to ignore.
If what he says is true,	If what I say is true,
'Tis death to marry you!	'Tis death to marry you!
Here's a pretty state of things!	Here's a pretty state of things!
Here's a pretty how-de-do!	Here's a pretty how-de-do!

[*Exeunt* YUM-YUM.

KO. (*going up to* NANKI-POO). My poor boy, I'm really sorry for you.

NANK. Thanks, old fellow. I'm sure you are.

KO. You see I'm quite helpless.

NANK. I quite see that.

KO. I can't conceive anything more distressing than to have one's marriage broken off at the last moment. But you shan't be disappointed of a wedding—you shall come to mine.

NANK. It's awfully kind of you, but that's impossible.

KO. Why so?

NANK. To-day I die.

KO. What do you mean?

NANK. I can't live without Yum-Yum. This afternoon I perform the Happy Despatch.

KO. No, no—pardon me—I can't allow that.

NANK. Why not?

KO. Why, hang it all, you're under contract to die by the hand of the Police Executioner in a month's time! If you kill yourself, what's to become of me? Why, I shall have to be executed in your place!

NANK. It would certainly seem so!

Enter POOH-BAH

KO. Now then, Lord Mayor, what is it?

POOH. The Mikado and his suite are approaching the city, and will be here in ten minutes.

KO. The Mikado! He's coming to see whether his orders have been carried out! (*To* NANKI-POO.) Now look here, you know—this is getting serious—a bargain's a bargain, and you really mustn't frustrate the ends of justice by committing suicide. As a man of honour and a gentleman, you are bound to die ignominiously by the hands of the Public Executioner.

NANK. Very well, then—behead me.

KO. What, now?

NANK. Certainly; at once.

POOH. Chop it off! Chop it off!

KO. My good sir, I don't go about prepared to execute gentlemen at a moment's notice. Why, I never even killed a blue-bottle!

POOH. Still, as Lord High Executioner—

KO. My good sir, as Lord High Executioner, I've got to behead him in a month. I'm not ready yet. I don't know how it's done. I'm going to take lessons. I mean to begin with a guinea pig, and work my way through the animal kingdom till I come to a Second Trombone. Why, you don't suppose that, as a humane man, I'd have accepted the post of Lord High Executioner if I hadn't thought the duties were purely nominal? I *can't* kill you—I can't kill anything! I can't kill anybody! (*Weeps.*)

NANK. Come, my poor fellow, we all have unpleasant duties to discharge at times; after all, what is it? If I don't mind, why should you? Remember, sooner or later it must be done.

KO. (*springing up suddenly*). *Must it?* I'm not so sure about that!

NANK. What do you mean?

KO. Why should I kill you when making an affidavit that you've been executed will do just as well? Here are plenty of witnesses—the Lord Chief Justice, Lord High Admiral, Commander-in-Chief, Secretary of State for the Home Department, First Lord of the Treasury, and Chief Commissioner of Police.

NANK. But where are they?

KO. There they are. They'll all swear to it—won't you? (*To* POOH-BAH.)

POOH. Am I to understand that all of us high Officers of State are required to perjure ourselves to ensure your safety?

KO. Why not? You'll be grossly insulted, as usual.

POOH. Will the insult be cash down, or at a date?

KO. It will be a ready-money transaction.

POOH. (*Aside.*) Well, it will be a useful discipline. (*Aloud.*) Very good. Choose your fiction, and I'll endorse it! (*Aside.*) Ha! ha! Family Pride, how do you like *that,* my buck?

NANK. But I tell you that life without Yum-Yum—

KO. Oh, Yum-Yum, Yum-Yum! Bother Yum-Yum! Here, Commissionaire (*to* POOH-BAH), go and fetch Yum-Yum. (*Exit* POOH-BAH.) Take Yum-Yum and marry Yum-Yum, only go away and never come back again. (*Enter* POOH-BAH *with* YUM-YUM.) Here she is. Yum-Yum, are you particularly busy?

YUM. Not particularly.

KO. You've five minutes to spare?

YUM. Yes.

KO. Then go along with his Grace the Archbishop of Titipu; he'll marry you at once.

YUM. But if I'm to be buried alive?

KO. Now, don't ask any questions, but do as I tell you, and Nanki-Poo will explain all.

NANK. But one moment—

KO. Not for worlds. Here comes the Mikado, no doubt to ascertain whether I've obeyed his decree, and if he finds you alive I shall have the greatest difficulty in persuading him that I've beheaded you. (*Exeunt* NANKI-POO *and* YUM-YUM, *followed by* POOH-BAH.) Close thing that, for here he comes!

[*Exit* KO-KO.

March.—Enter procession, heralding MIKADO,
with KATISHA

Entrance of MIKADO *and* KATISHA

(*"March of the Mikado's troops."*)

CHORUS.
　　Miya sama, miya sama,
　　On n'm-ma no mayé ni
　　Pira-Pira suru no wa
　　Nan gia na
　　Toko tonyaré tonyaré na?

DUET—MIKADO *and* KATISHA

MIK.
　From every kind of man
　　Obedience I expect;
　I'm the Emperor of Japan—

KAT.
　And I'm his daughter-in-law elect!
　　He'll marry his son
　　(He's only got one)
　To his daughter-in-law elect.

MIK.
　My morals have been declared
　　Particularly correct;

KAT.
　But they're nothing at all, compared
　　With those of his daughter-in-law elect!
　　　Bow—Bow—
　　To his daughter-in-law elect!

ALL.
　　　Bow—Bow—
　　To his daughter-in-law elect.

MIK.
　In a fatherly kind of way
　　I govern each tribe and sect,
　All cheerfully own my sway—

KAT.
　Except his daughter-in-law elect!
　　As tough as a bone,

My object all sublime / I shall achieve in time— / To let the punishment fit the crime—

With a will of her own,
Is his daughter-in-law elect!

MIK. My nature is love and light—
My freedom from all defect—

KAT. Is insignificant quite,
Compared with his daughter-in-law elect!
Bow—Bow—
To his daughter-in-law elect!

ALL. Bow—Bow—
To his daughter-in-law elect!

SONG—MIKADO *and* CHORUS

A more humane Mikado never
Did in Japan exist,
To nobody second,
I'm certainly reckoned
A true philanthropist.
It is my very humane endeavour
To make, to some extent,
Each evil liver
A running river
Of harmless merriment.

My object all sublime
I shall achieve in time—
To let the punishment fit the crime—
The punishment fit the crime;
And make each prisoner pent
Unwillingly represent
A source of innocent merriment!
Of innocent merriment!

All prosy dull society sinners,
Who chatter and bleat and bore,
Are sent to hear sermons
From mystical Germans
Who preach from ten till four.
The amateur tenor, whose vocal villainies
All desire to shirk,
Shall, during off-hours,
Exhibit his powers
To Madame Tussaud's waxwork.

The lady who dyes a chemical yellow
Or stains her grey hair puce,
Or pinches her figger,
Is painted with vigour.
With permanent walnut juice
The idiot who, in railway carriages,
Scribbles on window-panes,
We only suffer
To ride on a buffer
In Parliamentary trains.

My object all sublime, etc.

CHORUS. His object all sublime, etc.

The advertising quack who wearies
With tales of countless cures,
His teeth, I've enacted,
Shall all be extracted
By terrified amateurs.
The music-hall singer attends a series
Of masses and fugues and "ops"
By Bach, interwoven
With Spohr and Beethoven,
At classical Monday Pops.

The billiard sharp whom any one catches,
His doom's extremely hard—
He's made to dwell—
In a dungeon cell
On a spot that's always barred.
And there he plays extravagant matches
In fitless finger-stalls
On a cloth untrue,
With a twisted cue
And elliptical billiard balls!

My object all sublime, etc.

CHORUS. His object all sublime, etc.

Enter POOH-BAH, KO-KO, *and* PITTI-SING. *All kneel*

(POOH-BAH *hands a paper to* KO-KO.)

KO. I am honoured in being permitted to welcome your Majesty. I guess the object of your Majesty's visit—your wishes have been attended to. The execution has taken place.

MIK. Oh, you've had an execution, have you?

KO. Yes. The Coroner has just handed me his certificate.

POOH. I am the Coroner. (KO-KO *hands certificate to* MIKADO.)

MIK. And this is the certificate of his death. (*Reads.*) "At Titipu, in the presence of the Lord Chancellor, Lord Chief Justice, Attorney-General, Secretary of State for the Home Department, Lord Mayor, and Groom of the Second Floor Front—"

POOH. They were all present, your Majesty. I counted them myself.

MIK. Very good house. I wish I'd been in time for the performance.

KO. A tough fellow he was, too—a man of gigantic strength. His struggles were terrific. It was really a remarkable scene.

MIK. Describe it.

TRIO AND CHORUS
KO-KO, PITTI-SING, POOH-BAH *and* CHORUS

KO. The criminal cried, as he dropped him down,
In a state of wild alarm—
With a frightful, frantic, fearful frown,

I bared my big right arm.
I seized him by his little pig-tail,
And on his knees fell he,
  As he squirmed and struggled,
  And gurgled and guggled,
I drew my snickersnee!
  Oh, never shall I
  Forget the cry,
Or the shriek that shriekèd he,
  As I gnashed my teeth,
  When from its sheath
I drew my snickersnee!

CHORUS

We know him well,
He cannot tell
Untrue or groundless tales—
  He always tries
  To utter lies,
And every time he fails.

PITTI. He shivered and shook as he gave the sign
  For the stroke he didn't deserve;
When all of a sudden his eye met mine,
  And it seemed to brace his nerve;
For he nodded his head and kissed his hand,
  And he whistled an air, did he,
  As the sabre true
  Cut cleanly through
His cervical vertebrae!
  When a man's afraid,
  A beautiful maid
Is a cheering sight to see;
  And it's oh, I'm glad
  That moment sad
Was soothed by sight of me!

CHORUS

Her terrible tale
You can't assail,
With truth it quite agrees:
  Her taste exact
  For faultless fact
Amounts to a disease.

POOH. Now though you'd have said that head was dead
  (For its owner dead was he),
It stood on its neck, with a smile well-bred,
  And bowed three times to me!
It was none of your impudent off-hand nods,
  But as humble as could be;
  For it clearly knew
  The deference due
To a man of pedigree!
  And it's oh, I vow,

This deathly bow
Was a touching sight to see;
  Though trunkless, yet
  It couldn't forget
The deference due to me!

CHORUS

This haughty youth,
He speaks the truth
Whenever he finds it pays:
  And in this case
  It all took place
Exactly as he says!

[*Exeunt* CHORUS.

MIK. All this is very interesting, and I should like to have seen it. But we came about a totally different matter. A year ago my son, the heir to the throne of Japan, bolted from our Imperial Court.

KO. Indeed! Had he any reason to be dissatisfied with his position?

KAT. None whatever. On the contrary, I was going to marry him—yet he fled!

POOH. I am surprised that he should have fled from one so lovely!

KAT. That's not true.

POOH. No!

KAT. You hold that I am not beautiful because my face is plain. But you know nothing; you are still unenlightened. Learn, then, that it is not in the face alone that beauty is to be sought. My face is unattractive!

POOH. It is.

KAT. But I have a left shoulder-blade that is a miracle of loveliness. People come miles to see it. My right elbow has a fascination that few can resist.

POOH. Allow me!

KAT. It is on view Tuesdays and Fridays, on presentation of visiting card. As for my circulation, it is the largest in the world.

KO. And yet he fled!

MIK. And is now masquerading in this town, disguised as a Second Trombone.

KO.
POOH. } A Second Trombone!
PITTI.

MIK. Yes; would it be troubling you too much if I asked you to produce him? He goes by the name of—

KAT. Nanki-Poo.

MIK. Nanki-Poo.

KO. It's quite easy. That is, it's rather difficult. In point of fact, he's gone abroad!

MIK. Gone abroad! His address.

KO. Knightsbridge!

KAT. (*who is reading certificate of death*). Ha!

MIK. What's the matter?

KAT. See here—his name—Nanki-Poo—beheaded this morning. Oh, where shall I find another? Where shall I find another?

[KO-KO, POOH-BAH, *and* PITTI-SING *fall on their knees.*

MIK. (*looking at paper*). Dear, dear, dear! this is very tiresome. (*To* KO-KO.) My poor fellow, in your anxiety to carry out my wishes you have beheaded the heir to the throne of Japan!

KO. I beg to offer an unqualified apology.

POOH. I desire to associate myself with that expression of regret.

PITTI. We really hadn't the least notion—

MIK. Of course you hadn't. How could you? Come, come, my good fellow, don't distress yourself—it was no fault of yours. If a man of exalted rank chooses to disguise himself as a Second Trombone, he must take the consequences. It really distresses me to see you take on so. I've no doubt he thoroughly deserved all he got. (*They rise.*)

KO. We are infinitely obliged to your Majesty—

PITTI. Much obliged, your Majesty.

POOH. Very much obliged, your Majesty.

MIK. Obliged? not a bit. Don't mention it. How *could* you tell?

POOH. No, of course we couldn't tell who the gentleman really was.

PITTI. It wasn't written on his forehead, you know.

KO. It might have been on his pocket-handkerchief, but Japanese don't use pocket-handkerchiefs! Ha! ha! ha!

MIK. Ha! ha! ha! (*To* KATISHA.) I forget the punishment for compassing the death of the Heir Apparent.

KO.
POOH. } Punishment. (*They drop down on their knees again.*)
PITTI.

MIK. Yes. Something lingering, with boiling oil in it, I fancy. Something of that sort. I think boiling oil occurs in it, but I'm not sure. I know it's something humorous, but lingering, with either boiling oil or melted lead. Come, come, don't fret—I'm not a bit angry.

KO. (*in abject terror*). If your Majesty will accept our assurance, we had no idea—

MIK. Of course—

PITTI. I knew nothing about it.

POOH. I wasn't there.

MIK. That's the pathetic part of it. Unfortunately, the fool of an Act says "compassing the death of the Heir Apparent." There's not a word about a mistake—

KO., PITTI., *and* POOH. No!

MIK. Or not knowing—

KO. No!

MIK. Or having no notion—

PITTI. No!

MIK. Or not being there—

POOH. No!

MIK. There should be, of course—

KO., PITTI., *and* POOH. Yes!

MIK. But there isn't.

KO., PITTI., *and* POOH. Oh!

MIK. That's the slovenly way in which these Acts are always drawn. However, cheer up, it'll be all right. I'll have it altered next session. Now, let's see about your execution—will after luncheon suit you? Can you wait till then?

KO., PITTI., *and* POOH. Oh, yes—we can wait till then!

MIK. Then we'll make it after luncheon.

POOH. I don't want any lunch.

MIK. I'm really very sorry for you all, but it's an unjust world, and virtue is triumphant only in theatrical performances.

GLEE
PITTI-SING, KATISHA, KO-KO, POOH-BAH, *and* MIKADO

MIK.   See how the Fates their gifts allot,
For A is happy—B is not.
Yet B is worthy, I dare say,
Of more prosperity than A!

KO., POOH., *and* PITTI. *Is* B more worthy?

KAT.   I should say
He's worth a great deal more than A.

ENSEMBLE. {
Yet A is happy!
Oh, so happy!
Laughing, Ha! ha!
Chaffing, Ha! ha!
Nectar quaffing, Ha! ha! ha!
Ever joyous, ever gay,
Happy, undeserving A!

KO., POOH., *and* PITTI.
If I were Fortune—which I'm not—
B should enjoy A's happy lot,
And A should die in miserie—
That is, assuming I am B.

MIK. *and* KAT.   But *should* A perish?

KO., POOH., *and* PITTI.   That should he
(Of course, assuming I am B).
B should be happy!
Oh, so happy!
Laughing, Ha! ha!
Chaffing, Ha! ha!
Nectar quaffing, Ha! ha! ha!
But condemned to die is he,
Wretched meritorious B!

[*Exeunt* MIKADO *and* KATISHA.

KO. Well, a nice mess you've got us into, with your nodding head and the deference due to a man of pedigree!

POOH. Merely corroborative detail, intended to give artistic verisimilitude to an otherwise bald and unconvincing narrative.

PITTI. Corroborative detail indeed! Corroborative fiddlestick!

There is beauty in the bellow of the blast, . . .

KO. And you're just as bad as he is with your cock-and-a-bull stories about catching his eye and his whistling an air. But that's so like you! You must put in your oar!

POOH. But how about your big right arm?

PITTI. Yes, and your snickersnee!

KO. Well, well, never mind that now. There's only one thing to be done. Nanki-Poo hasn't started yet—he must come to life again at once. (*Enter* NANKI-POO *and* YUM-YUM *prepared for journey.*) Here he comes. Here, Nanki-Poo, I've good news for you—you're reprieved.

NANK. Oh, but it's too late. I'm a dead man, and I'm off for my honeymoon.

KO. Nonsense! A terrible thing has just happened. It seems you're the son of the Mikado.

NANK. Yes, but that happened some time ago.

KO. Is this a time for airy persiflage? Your father is here, and with Katisha!

NANK. My father! And with Katisha!

KO. Yes, he wants you particularly.

POOH. So does she.

YUM. Oh, but he's married now.

KO. But, bless my heart! what has that to do with it?

NANK. Katisha claims me in marriage, but I can't marry her because I'm married already—consequently she will insist on my execution, and if I'm executed, my wife will have to be buried alive.

YUM. You see our difficulty.

KO. Yes. I don't know what's to be done.

NANK. There's one chance for you. If you could persuade Katisha to marry you, she would have no further claim on me, and in that case I could come to life without any fear of being put to death.

KO. I marry Katisha!

YUM. I really think it's the only course.

KO. But, my good girl, have you seen her? She's something appalling!

PITTI. Ah! that's only her face. She has a left elbow which people come miles to see!

POOH. I am told that her right heel is much admired by connoisseurs.

KO. My good sir, I decline to pin my heart upon any lady's right heel.

NANK. It comes to this: While Katisha is single, I prefer to be a disembodied spirit. When Katisha is married, existence will be as welcome as the flowers in spring.

DUET—NANKI-POO *and* KO-KO
(*With* YUM-YUM, PITTI-SING, *and* POOH-BAH)

NANK. The flowers that bloom in the spring,
    Tra la,
  Breathe promise of merry sunshine—
  As we merrily dance and we sing,
    Tra la,
  We welcome the hope that they bring,
    Tra la,

Of a summer of roses and wine.
  And that's what we mean when we say that a thing
  Is welcome as flowers that bloom in the spring.
    Tra la la la la la, etc.

ALL.   Tra la la la, etc.

KO.   The flowers that bloom in the spring,
    Tra la,
  Have nothing to do with the case.
I've got to take under my wing,
    Tra la,
A most unattractive old thing,
    Tra la,
  With a caricature of a face
  And that's what I mean when I say, or I sing,
  "Oh, bother the flowers that bloom in the spring."
    Tra la la la la la, etc.

ALL.   Tra la la la, Tra la la la, etc.
      [*Dance and exeunt* NANKI-POO, YUM-YUM,
      POOH-BAH, PITTI-SING, *and* KO-KO.

Enter KATISHA

RECITATIVE *and* SONG—KATISHA

Alone, and yet alive! Oh, sepulchre!
My soul is still my body's prisoner!
Remote the peace that Death alone can give—
My doom, to wait! my punishment, to live!

SONG

  Hearts do not break!
  They sting and ache
  For old love's sake,
    But do not die,
  Though with each breath
  They long for death
  As witnesseth
    The living I!
      Oh, living I!
      Come, tell me why,
      When hope is gone,
      Dost thou stay on?
      Why linger here,
      Where all is drear?
      Oh, living I!
      Come, tell me why,
      When hope is gone,
      Dost thou stay on?
    May not a cheated maiden die?

KO. (*entering and approaching her timidly*). Katisha!

KAT. The miscreant who robbed me of my love! But vengeance pursues—they are heating the cauldron!

KO. Katisha—behold a suppliant at your feet! Katisha—mercy!

KAT. Mercy? Had you mercy on him? See here, you! You have slain my love. He did not love *me*, but he would have loved me in time. I am an acquired taste—only the educated palate can appreciate *me*. I was educating *his* palate when he left me. Well, he is dead, and where shall I find another? It takes years to train a man to love me. Am I to go through the weary round again, and, at the same time, implore mercy for you who robbed me of my prey—I mean my pupil—just as his education was on the point of completion? Oh, where shall I find another?

KO. (*suddenly, and with great vehemence*). Here!—Here!

KAT. What!!!

KO. (*with intense passion*). Katisha, for years I have loved you with a white-hot passion that is slowly but surely consuming my very vitals! Ah, shrink not from me! If there is aught of woman's mercy in your heart, turn not away from a love-sick suppliant whose every fibre thrills at your tiniest touch! True it is that, under a poor mask of disgust, I have endeavoured to conceal a passion whose inner fires are broiling the soul within me! But the fire will not be smothered—it defies all attempts at extinction, and, breaking forth, all the more eagerly for its long restraint, it declares itself in words that will not be weighed—that cannot be schooled—that should not be too severely criticised. Katisha, I dare not hope for your love—but I will not live without it! Darling!

KAT. You, whose hands still reek with the blood of my betrothed, dare to address words of passion to the woman you have so foully wronged!

KO. I do—accept my love, or I perish on the spot!

KAT. Go to! Who knows so well as I that no one ever yet died of a broken heart!

KO. You know not what you say. Listen!

SONG—KO-KO

On a tree by a river a little tom-tit
    Sang "Willow, titwillow, titwillow!"
And I said to him, "Dicky-bird, why do you sit
    Singing 'Willow, titwillow, titwillow'?"
"Is it weakness of intellect, birdie?" I cried,
"Or a rather tough worm in your little inside?"
With a shake of his poor little head, he replied,
    "Oh, willow, titwillow, titwillow!"

He slapped at his chest, as he sat on that bough,
    Singing "Willow, titwillow, titwillow!"
And a cold perspiration bespangled his brow,
    Oh, willow, titwillow, titwillow!
He sobbed and he sighed, and a gurgle he gave,
Then he plunged himself into the billowy wave,
And an echo arose from the suicide's grave—
    "Oh, willow, titwillow, titwillow!"

Now I feel just as sure as I'm sure that my name
    Isn't Willow, titwillow, titwillow,
That 'twas blighted affection that made him exclaim
    "Oh, willow, titwillow, titwillow!"

And if you remain callous and obdurate, I
Shall perish as he did, and you will know why,
Though I probably shall not exclaim as I die,
    "Oh, willow, titwillow, titwillow!"

        [*During this song* KATISHA *has been greatly affected, and at the end is almost in tears.*

KAT. (*whimpering*). Did he really die of love?

KO. He really did.

KAT. All on account of a cruel little hen?

KO. Yes.

KAT. Poor little chap!

KO. It's an affecting tale, and quite true. I knew the bird intimately.

KAT. Did you? He must have been very fond of her.

KO. His devotion was something extraordinary.

KAT. (*still whimpering*). Poor little chap! And—and if I refuse you, will you go and do the same?

KO. At once.

KAT. No, no—you mustn't! Anything but that! (*Falls on his breast.*) Oh, I'm a silly little goose!

KO. (*making a wry face*). You are!

KAT. And you won't hate me because I'm just a little teeny weeny wee bit bloodthirsty, will you?

KO. Hate you? Oh, Katisha! is there not beauty even in bloodthirstiness?

KAT. My idea exactly.

DUET—KATISHA *and* KO-KO

KAT.   There is beauty in the bellow of the blast,
        There is grandeur in the growling of the gale,
            There is eloquent outpouring
            When the lion is a-roaring,
        And the tiger is a-lashing of his tail!

KO.   Yes, I like to see a tiger
        From the Congo or the Niger,
    And especially when lashing of his tail!

KAT.   Volcanoes have a splendour that is grim,
        And earthquakes only terrify the dolts,
        But to him who's scientific
            There's nothing that's terrific
        In the falling of a flight of thunderbolts!

KO.   Yes, in spite of all my meekness,
        If I have a little weakness,
    It's a passion for a flight of thunderbolts!

BOTH.   If that is so,
        Sing derry down derry!
       It's evident, very,
         Our tastes are one.
    Away we'll go,
       And merrily marry,
       Nor tardily tarry
         Till day is done!

KO.   There is beauty in extreme old age—

Do you fancy you are elderly enough?
    Information I'm requesting
    On a subject interesting:
Is a maiden all the better when she's tough?

KAT.   Throughout this wide dominion
    It's the general opinion
That she'll last a good deal longer when she's tough.

KO.   Are you old enough to marry, do you think?
    Won't you wait till you are eighty in the shade?
    There's a fascination frantic
    In a ruin that's romantic;
Do you think you are sufficiently decayed?

KAT.   To the matter that you mention
    I have given some attention,
And I think I am sufficiently decayed.

BOTH.   If that is so,
    Sing derry down derry!
    It's evident, very,
    Our tastes are one!
Away we'll go,
    And merrily marry,
    Nor tardily tarry
    Till day is done!

                [*Exeunt together.*

Flourish. Enter the MIKADO, *attended by* PISH-TUSH
and Court

MIK. Now then, we've had a capital lunch, and we're quite ready. Have all the painful preparations been made?

PISH. Your Majesty, all is prepared.

MIK. Then produce the unfortunate gentleman and his two well-meaning but misguided accomplices.

Enter KO-KO, KATISHA, POOH-BAH, *and* PITTI-SING.
They throw themselves at the MIKADO'S *feet.*

KAT. Mercy! Mercy for Ko-Ko! Mercy for Pitti-Sing! Mercy even for Pooh-Bah!

MIK. I beg your pardon, I don't think I quite caught that remark.

POOH. Mercy even for Pooh-Bah.

KAT. Mercy! My husband that was to have been is dead, and I have just married this miserable object.

MIK. Oh! You've not been long about it!

KO. We were married before the Registrar.

POOH. *I* am the Registrar.

MIK. I see. But my difficulty is that, as you have slain the Heir Apparent—

Enter NANKI-POOH *and* YUM-YUM. *They kneel*

NANKI. The Heir Apparent is *not* slain.

MIK. Bless my heart, my son!

YUM. And your daughter-in-law elected!

KAT. (*seizing* KO-KO). Traitor, you have deceived me!

MIK. Yes, you are entitled to a little explanation, but I think he will give it better whole than in pieces.

KO. Your Majesty, it's like this: It is true that I stated that I had killed Nanki-Poo—

MIK. Yes, with most affecting particulars.

POOH. Merely corroborative detail intended to give artistic verisimilitude to a bald and—

KO. *Will* you refrain from putting in your oar? (*To* MIKADO.) It's like this: When your Majesty says, "Let a thing be done," it's as good as done—practically, it *is* done—because your Majesty's will is law. Your Majesty says, "Kill a gentleman," and a gentleman is told off to be killed. Consequently, that gentleman is as good as dead—practically, he *is* dead—and if he is dead, why not say so?

MIK. I see. Nothing could possibly be more satisfactory!

FINALE

PITTI.   For he's gone and married Yum-Yum—

ALL.   Yum-Yum!

PITTI.   Your anger pray bury,
    For all will be merry,
I think you had better succumb—

ALL.   Cumb—cumb!

PITTI.   And join our expressions of glee!

KO.   On this subject I pray you be dumb—

ALL.   Dumb—dumb!

KO.   Your notions, though many,
    Are not worth a penny,
The word for your guidance is "Mum"—

ALL.   Mum—Mum!

KO.   You've a very good bargain in me.

ALL.   On this subject we pray you be dumb—
                  Dumb—dumb!
We think you had better succumb—
                  Cumb—cumb!

    You'll find there are many
    Who'll wed for a penny,
There are lots of good fish in the sea.

YUM. *and* NANK.   The threatened cloud has passed away,
    And brightly shines the dawning day;
    What though the night may come too soon,
    We've years and years of afternoon!

ALL.   Then let the throng
        Our joy advance,
    With laughing song
        And merry dance,
    With joyous shout and ringing cheer,
    Inaugurate our new career!
        Then let the throng, etc.

CURTAIN

THE GONDOLIERS

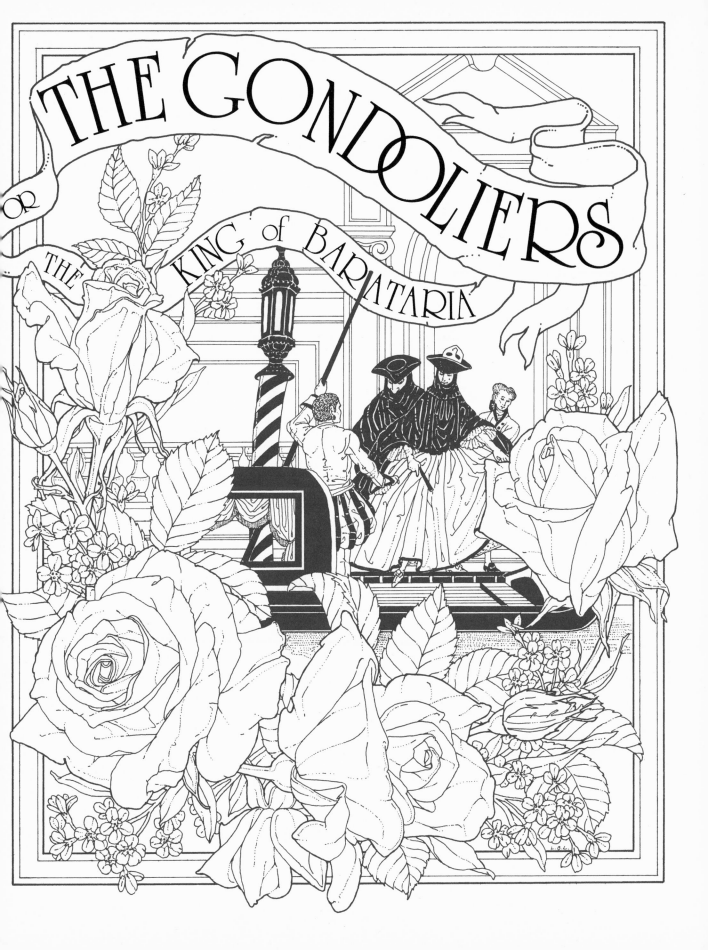

DRAMATIS PERSONÆ

THE DUKE OF PLAZA-TORO (*a Grandee of Spain*)

LUIZ (*his Attendant*)

DON ALHAMBRA DEL BOLERO (*the Grand Inquisitor*)

MARCO PALMIERI
GIUSEPPE PALMIERI
ANTONIO } (*Venetian Gondoliers*)
FRANCESCO
GIORGIO
ANNIBALE

THE DUCHESS OF PLAZA-TORO

CASILDA (*her Daughter*)

GIANETTA
TESSA
FIAMETTA } (*Contadine*)
VITTORIA
GIULIA

INEZ (*the King's Foster-mother*)

*Chorus of Gondoliers and Contadine, Men-at-Arms,
Heralds, and Pages*

ACT I

THE PIAZZETTA, VENICE

ACT II

PAVILION IN THE PALACE OF BARATARIA

(*An interval of three months is supposed to elapse
between Acts I and II*)

Date 1750

First produced at the Savoy Theatre on December 7, 1889

THE GONDOLIERS
OR, THE KING of BARATARIA

ACT I

SCENE.—*The Piazzetta, Venice. The Ducal Palace on the right.*

FIAMETTA, GIULIA, VITTORIA, *and other Contadine discovered, each tying a bouquet of roses*

CHORUS OF CONTADINE

List and learn, ye dainty roses,
    Roses white and roses red,
Why we bind you into posies
    Ere your morning bloom has fled
By a law of maiden's making,
Accents of a heart that's aching,
Even though that heart be breaking,
    Should by maiden be unsaid:
Though they love with love exceeding,
They must seem to be unheeding—
Go ye then and do their pleading,
    Roses white and roses red!

FIAMETTA

Two there are for whom in duty,
    Every maid in Venice sighs—
Two so peerless in their beauty
    That they shame the summer skies.
We have hearts for them, in plenty,
    They have hearts, but all too few,
We, alas, are four-and-twenty!
    They, alas, are only two!
We, alas!

CHORUS.   Alas!

FIA.   Are four-and-twenty,
       They, alas!

CHORUS.   Alas!

FIA.   Are only two.

CHORUS.   They, alas, are only two, alas!
       Now ye know, ye dainty roses,
       Why we bind you into posies,

Ere your morning bloom has fled,
Roses white and roses red!

[*During this chorus* ANTONIO, FRANCESCO, GIORGIO, *and other Gondoliers have entered unobserved by the Girls—at first two, then two more, then four, then half a dozen, then the remainder of the Chorus.*

SOLI

FRANC.   Good morrow, pretty maids; for whom prepare ye
        These floral tributes extraordinary?

FIA.   For Marco and Giuseppe Palmieri,
        The pink and flower of all the Gondolieri.

GIU.   They're coming here, as we have heard but lately,
        To choose two brides from us who sit sedately.

ANT.   Do all you maidens love them?

ALL.   Passionately!

ANT.   These gondoliers are to be envied greatly!

GIOR.   But what of us, who one and all adore you?
        Have pity on our passion, we implore you!

FIA.   These gentlemen must make their choice before you;

VIT.   In the meantime we tacitly ignore you.

GIU.   When they have chosen two that leaves you plenty—
        Two dozen we, and ye are four-and-twenty.

FIA. *and* VIT. Till then, enjoy your *dolce far niente.*

ANT.   With pleasure, nobody *contradicente!*

SONG—ANTONIO *and* CHORUS

For the merriest fellows are we, tra la,
That ply on the emerald sea, tra la;
    With loving and laughing,
    And quipping and quaffing,
We're happy as happy can be, tra la—
    As happy as happy can be!

With sorrow we've nothing to do, tra la,
And care is a thing to pooh-pooh, tra la;
    And Jealousy yellow,
    Unfortunate fellow,
We drown in the shimmering blue, tra la—
    We drown in the shimmering blue!

FIA. (*looking off*). See, see, at last they come to make their
            choice—
    Let us acclaim them with united voice.

[MARCO *and* GIUSEPPE *appear in gondola at back.*

CHORUS (*Girls*). Hail, hail! gallant gondolieri, ben' venuti!
    Accept our love, our homage, and our duty.

[MARCO *and* GIUSEPPE *jump ashore—the Girls*
        salute them.

DUET—MARCO *and* GIUSEPPE,
with CHORUS OF GIRLS

MAR. *and* GIU.   Buon' giorno, signorine!

GIRLS.   Gondolieri carissimi!
             Siamo contadine!

MAR. *and* GIU. (*bowing*). Servitori umilissimi!
             Per chi questi fiori—
             Questi fiori bellissimi?

GIRLS.   Per voi, bel' signori
             O eccellentissimi!

[*The Girls present their bouquets to* MARCO *and* GIUSEPPE, *who
are overwhelmed with them, and carry them with difficulty.*

MAR. *and* GIU. (*their arms full of flowers*). O ciel'!

GIRLS.   Buon' giorno, cavalieri!

MAR. *and* GIU. (*deprecatingly*).   Siamo gondolieri.

(*To* FIA. *and* VIT.)   Signorina, io t'amo!

GIRLS (*deprecatingly*).   Contadine siamo.

MAR. *and* GIU.   Signorine!

GIRLS (*deprecatingly*).   Contadine!

(*Curtseying to* MAR. *and* GIU.) Cavalieri.

MAR. *and* GIU. (*deprecatingly*).   Gondolieri!

             Poveri gondolieri!

CHORUS.   Buon' giorno, signorine, etc.

DUET—MARCO *and* GIUSEPPE

We're called *gondolieri,*
But that's a vagary,
It's quite honorary
    The trade that we ply.
For gallantry noted

Since we were short-coated,
To beauty devoted,
    Giuseppe ⎫
    Are Marco ⎬ and I;

When morning is breaking,
Our couches forsaking,
To greet their awaking
    With carols we come.
At summer day's nooning,
When weary lagooning,
Our mandolins tuning,
    We lazily thrum.

When vespers are ringing,
To hope ever clinging,
With songs of our singing
    A vigil we keep,
When daylight is fading,
Enwrapt in night's shading,
With soft serenading
    We sing them to sleep.

We're called *gondolieri,* etc.

RECITATIVE—MARCO *and* GIUSEPPE

MAR.   And now to choose our brides!

GIU.   As all are young and fair,
      And amiable besides,

BOTH.   We really do not care
      A preference to declare.

MAR.   A bias to disclose
      Would be indelicate—

GIU.   And therefore we propose
      To let impartial Fate
      Select for us a mate!

ALL.   Viva!

GIRLS.   A bias to disclose
      Would be indelicate—

MEN.   But how do they propose
      To let impartial Fate
      Select for them a mate?

GIU.   These handkerchiefs upon our eyes be good enough
      to bind,

MAR. And take good care that both of us are absolutely
      blind;

BOTH. Then turn us round—and we, with all convenient
      despatch,
      Will undertake to marry any two of you we catch!

ALL.   Viva!

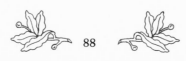

That highly respectable gondolier / Could never declare with a mind sincere / Which of the two was his offspring dear, . . .

They undertake to marry any two of {us they catch! / them they catch!

[*The Girls prepare to bind their eyes as directed.*

FIA. (*to* MARCO). Are you peeping?
Can you see me?

MAR. Dark I'm keeping,
Dark and dreamy!

(MARCO *slyly lifts bandage.*)

VIT. (*to* GIUSEPPE). If you're blinded
Truly, say so.

GIU. All right-minded
Players play so! (*slyly lifts bandage*)

FIA. (*detecting* MARCO). Conduct shady!
They are cheating!
Surely they de-
Serve a beating! (*replaces bandage*)

VIT. (*detecting* GIUSEPPE).
This too much is;
Maidens mocking—
Conduct such is
Truly shocking! (*replaces bandage*)

ALL. You can spy, sir!
Shut your eye, sir!
You may use it by and by, sir!
You can see, sir!
Don't tell me, sir!
That will do—now let it be, sir!

CHORUS OF My papa he keeps three horses,
GIRLS. Black, and white, and dapple grey, sir;
Turn three times, then take your courses,
Catch whichever girl you may, sir!

CHORUS OF MEN. My papa, etc.

[MARCO *and* GIUSEPPE *turn round, as directed, and try to catch the girls. Business of blind-man's buff. Eventually* MARCO *catches* GIANETTA, *and* GIUSEPPE *catches* TESSA. *The two girls try to escape, but in vain. The two men pass their hands over the girls' faces to discover their identity.*

GIU. I've at length achieved a capture!
(*Guessing.*) This is Tessa! (*removes bandage*) Rapture, rapture!

MAR. (*guessing*). To me Gianetta fate has granted!
(*removes bandage*)
Just the very girl I wanted!

GIU. (*politely to* MAR.). If you'd rather change—
TESS. My goodness!
This indeed is simple rudeness.

MAR. (*politely to* GIU.). I've no preference whatever—

GIA. Listen to him! Well, I never!
(*Each man kisses each girl.*)

GIA. Thank you, gallant *gondolieri!*
In a set and formal measure
It is scarcely necessary
To express our pleasure.
Each of us to prove a treasure,
Conjugal and monetary,
Gladly will devote our leisure,
Gay and gallant *gondolieri.*
Tra, la, la, la, la, la, etc.

TESS. Gay and gallant *gondolieri,*
Take us both and hold us tightly,
You have luck extraordinary;
We might both have been unsightly!
If we judge your conduct rightly,
'Twas a choice involuntary;
Still we thank you most politely,
Gay and gallant *gondolieri!*
Tra, la, la, la, la, la, etc.

CHORUS OF Thank you, gallant *gondolieri;*
GIRLS In a set and formal measure,
It is scarcely necessary
To express our pleasure.
Each of us to prove a treasure
Gladly will devote our leisure,
Gay and gallant *gondolieri!*
Tra, la, la, la, la, la, etc.

ALL. Fate in this has put his finger—
Let us bow to Fate's decree,
Then no longer let us linger,
To the altar hurry we!

[*They all dance off two and two—*GIANETTA *with* MARCO, TESSA *with* GIUSEPPE.

Flourish. A gondola arrives at the Piazzetta steps, from which enter the DUKE OF PLAZA-TORO, *the* DUCHESS, *their daughter* CASILDA, *and their attendant* LUIZ, *who carries a drum. All are dressed in pompous but old and faded clothes.*

Entrance of DUKE, DUCHESS, CASILDA, *and* LUIZ

DUKE. From the sunny Spanish shore,
The Duke of Plaza-Tor!—

DUCH. And His Grace's Duchess true—

CAS. And His Grace's daughter, too—

LUIZ. And His Grace's private drum
To Venetia's shores have come:

ALL. If ever, ever, ever
They get back to Spain,
They will never, never, never
Cross the sea again—

90

DUKE.   Neither that Grandee from the Spanish shore,
           The noble Duke of Plaza Tor'–

DUCH.   Nor His Grace's Duchess, staunch and true–

CAS.   You may add, His Grace's daughter, too–

LUIZ.   Nor His Grace's own particular drum
           To Venetia's shores will come:

ALL.   If ever, ever, ever
              They get back to Spain,
          They will never, never, never
             Cross the sea again!

DUKE. At last we have arrived at our destination. This is the Ducal Palace, and it is here that the Grand Inquisitor resides. As a Castilian hidalgo of ninety-five quarterings, I regret that I am unable to pay my state visit on a horse. As a Castilian hidalgo of that description, I should have preferred to ride through the streets of Venice; but owing, I presume, to an unusually wet season, the streets are in such a condition that equestrian exercise is impracticable. No matter. Where is our suite?

LUIZ (*coming forward*). Your Grace, I am here.

DUCH. Why do you not do yourself the honour to kneel when you address His Grace?

DUKE. My love, it is so small a matter! (*To* LUIZ.) Still, you may as well do it. (LUIZ *kneels.*)

CAS. The young man seems to entertain but an imperfect appreciation of the respect due from a menial to a Castilian hidalgo.

DUKE. My child, you are hard upon our suite.

CAS. Papa, I've no patience with the presumption of persons in his plebian position. If he does not appreciate that position, let him be whipped until he does.

DUKE. Let us hope the omission was not intended as a slight. I should be much hurt if I thought it was. So would he. (*To* LUIZ.) Where are the halberdiers who were to have had the honour of meeting us here, that our visit to the Grand Inquisitor might be made in becoming state?

LUIZ. Your Grace, the halberdiers are mercenary people who stipulated for a trifle on account.

DUKE. How tiresome! Well, let us hope the Grand Inquisitor is a blind gentleman. And the band who were to have had the honour of escorting us? I see no band!

LUIZ. Your Grace, the band are sordid persons who required to be paid in advance.

DUCH. That's so like a band!

DUKE (*annoyed*). Insuperable difficulties meet me at every turn!

DUCH. But surely they know His Grace?

LUIZ. Exactly–they know His Grace.

DUKE. Well, let us hope that the Grand Inquisitor is a deaf gentleman. A cornet-à-piston would be something. You do not happen to possess the accomplishment of tootling like a cornet-à-piston?

LUIZ. Alas, no, Your Grace! But I can imitate a farmyard.

DUKE (*doubtfully*). I don't see how that would help us. I don't see how we could bring it in.

CAS. It would not help us in the least. We are not a parcel of graziers come to market, dolt!

DUKE. My love, our suite's feelings! (*To* LUIZ.) Be so good as to ring the bell and inform the Grand Inquisitor that his Grace the Duke of Plaza-Toro, Count Matadoro, Baron Picadoro–

DUCH. And suite–

DUKE. And suite–have arrived at Venice, and seek–

CAS. Desire–

DUCH. Demand!

DUKE. And demand an audience.

LUIZ. Your Grace has but to command. (*Rising.*)

DUKE (*much moved*). I felt sure of it–I felt sure of it! (*Exit* LUIZ *into Ducal Palace.*) And now my love–(*aside to* DUCHESS) Shall we tell her? I think so–(*aloud to* CASILDA) And now, my love, prepare for a magnificent surprise. It is my agreeable duty to reveal to you a secret which should make you the happiest young lady in Venice!

CAS. A secret?

DUCH. A secret which, for state reasons, it has been necessary to preserve for twenty years.

DUKE. When you were a prattling babe of six months old you were married by proxy to no less a personage than the infant son and heir of His Majesty the immeasurably wealthy King of Barataria!

CAS. Married to the infant son of the King of Barataria? Was I consulted? (DUKE *shakes his head.*) Then it was a most unpardonable liberty!

DUKE. Consider his extreme youth and forgive him. Shortly after the ceremony that misguided monarch abandoned the creed of his forefathers, and became a Wesleyan Methodist of the most bigoted and persecuting type. The Grand Inquisitor, determined that the innovation should not be perpetuated in Barataria, caused your smiling and unconscious husband to be stolen and conveyed to Venice. A fortnight since the Methodist Monarch and all his Wesleyan Court were killed in an insurrection, and we are here to ascertain the whereabouts of your husband, and to hail you, our daughter, as Her Majesty, the reigning Queen of Barataria! (*Kneels.*)

During this speech LUIZ *re-enters*

DUCH. Your Majesty! (*Kneels.*)

DUKE. It is at such moments as these that one feels how necessary it is to travel with a full band.

CAS. I, the Queen of Barataria! But I've nothing to wear! We are practically penniless!

DUKE. That point has not escaped me. Although I am unhappily in straitened circumstances at present, my social influence is something enormous; and a Company, to be called the Duke of Plaza-Toro, Limited, is in course of formation to work me. An influential directorate has been secured, and I shall myself join the Board after allotment.

CAS. Am I to understand that the Queen of Barataria may be called upon at any time to witness her honoured sire in process of liquidation?

DUCH. The speculation is not exempt from that drawback. If your father should stop, it will, of course, be necessary to wind him up.

CAS. But it's so undignified—it's so degrading! A Grandee of Spain turned into a public company? Such a thing was never heard of!

DUKE. My child, the Duke of Plaza-Toro does not follow fashions—he leads them. He always leads everybody. When he was in the army he led his regiment. He occasionally led them into action. He invariably led them out of it.

SONG—DUKE OF PLAZA-TORO

In enterprise of martial kind,
    When there was any fighting,
He led his regiment from behind—
    He found it less exciting.
But when away his regiment ran,
    His place was at the fore, O—
        That celebrated,
        Cultivated,
        Underrated
            Nobleman,
        The Duke of Plaza-Toro!

ALL.   In the first and foremost flight, ha, ha!
    You always found that knight, ha, ha!
        That celebrated,
        Cultivated,
        Underrated
            Nobleman,
        The Duke of Plaza-Toro!

DUKE.   When, to evade Destruction's hand,
        To hide they all proceeded,
    No soldier in that gallant band
        Hid half as well as he did.
    He lay concealed throughout the war,
        And so preserved his gore, O!
            That unaffected,
            Undetected,
            Well-connected
                Warrior,
            The Duke of Plaza-Toro!

ALL.   In every doughty deed, ha, ha!
    He always took the lead, ha, ha!
        That unaffected,
        Undetected,
        Well-connected
            Warrior,
        The Duke of Plaza-Toro!

DUKE.   When told that they would all be shot
        Unless they left the service,

That hero hesitated not,
        So marvellous his nerve is.
    He sent his resignation in,
        The first of all his corps, O!
            That very knowing,
            Overflowing,
            Easy-going
                Paladin,
            The Duke of Plaza-Toro!

ALL.   To men of grosser clay, ha, ha!
    He always showed the way, ha, ha!
        That very knowing,
        Overflowing,
        Easy-going
            Paladin,
        The Duke of Plaza-Toro!

[*Exeunt* DUKE *and* DUCHESS *into Grand Ducal Palace. As soon as they have disappeared,* LUIZ *and* CASILDA *rush to each other's arms.*

RECITATIVE AND DUET—CASILDA *and* LUIZ

O rapture, when alone together
    Two loving hearts and those that bear them
May join in temporary tether,
    Though Fate apart should rudely tear them.

CAS.   Necessity, Invention's mother,
        Compelled me to a course of feigning—
    But, left alone with one another,
        I will atone for my disdaining!

            Ah, well-beloved,
            Mine angry frown
            Is but a gown
            That serves to dress
            My gentleness!

LUIZ.   Ah, well-beloved,
            Thy cold disdain,
            It gives no pain—
            'Tis mercy, played
            In masquerade!

BOTH.   Ah, well-beloved, etc.

CAS. O Luiz, Luiz—what have you said? What have I done? What have I allowed you to do?

LUIZ. Nothing, I trust, that you will ever have reason to repent. (*Offering to embrace her.*)

CAS. (*withdrawing from him*). Nay, Luiz, it may not be. I have embraced you for the last time.

LUIZ (*amazed*). Casilda!

CAS. I have just learnt, to my surprise and indignation, that I was wed in babyhood to the infant son of the King of Barataria!

LUIZ. The son of the King of Barataria? The child who was stolen in infancy by the Inquisition?

Oh, 'tis a glorious thing, I ween, / To be a regular Royal Queen!

CAS. The same. But of course, you know his story.

LUIZ. Know his story? Why, I have often told you that my mother was the nurse to whose charge he was entrusted!

CAS. True. I had forgotten. Well, he has been discovered, and my father has brought me here to claim his hand.

LUIZ. But you will not recognize this marriage? It took place when you were too young to understand its import.

CAS. Nay, Luiz, respect my principles and cease to torture me with vain entreaties. Henceforth my life is another's.

LUIZ. But stay—the present and the future—*they* are another's; but the past—that at least is ours, and none can take it from us. As we may revel in naught else, let us revel in that!

CAS. I don't think I grasp your meaning.

LUIZ. Yet it is logical enough. You say you cease to love me?

CAS. (*demurely*). I say I *may* not love you.

LUIZ. Ah, but you do not say you *did* not love me?

CAS. I loved you with a frenzy that words are powerless to express—and that but ten brief minutes since!

LUIZ. Exactly. My own—that is, until ten minutes since, my own—my lately loved, my recently adored—tell me that until, say a quarter of an hour ago, I was all in all to thee! (*Embracing her.*)

CAS. I see your idea. It's ingenious, but don't do that. (*Releasing herself.*)

LUIZ. There can be no harm in revelling in the past.

CAS. None whatever, but an embrace cannot be taken to act retrospectively.

LUIZ. Perhaps not!

CAS. We may recollect an embrace—I recollect many—but we must not repeat them.

LUIZ. Then let us recollect a few! (*A moment's pause, as they recollect, then both heave a deep sigh.*)

LUIZ. Ah, Casilda, you were to me as the sun is to the earth!

CAS. A quarter of an hour ago?

LUIZ. About that.

CAS. And to think that, but for this miserable discovery, you would have been my own for life!

LUIZ. Through life to death—a quarter of an hour ago!

CAS. How greedily my thirsty ears would have drunk the golden melody of those sweet words a quarter—well, it's now about twenty minutes since. (*Looking at her watch.*)

LUIZ. About that. In such a matter one cannot be too precise.

CAS. And now our love, so full of life, is but a silent, solemn memory!

LUIZ. Must it be so, Casilda?

CAS. Luiz, it must be so!

DUET—CASILDA *and* LUIZ

LUIZ.　　　There was a time—
　　　　　　A time for ever gone—ah, woe is me!
　　　　It was no crime
　　　　　　To love but thee alone—ah, woe is me!

　　　　　　One heart, one life, one soul,
　　　　　　　　One aim, one goal—
　　　　　　Each in the other's thrall,
　　　　　　　　Each all in all, ah, woe is me!

BOTH.　Oh, bury, bury—let the grave close o'er
　　　　The days that were—that never will be more!
　　　　Oh, bury, bury love that all condemn,
　　　　And let the whirlwind mourn its requiem!

CAS.　　　Dead as the last year's leaves—
　　　　　　　As gathered flowers—ah, woe is me!
　　　　Dead as the garnered sheaves,
　　　　　　　That love of ours—ah, woe is me!
　　　　Born but to fade and die
　　　　　　When hope was high,
　　　　Dead and as far away
　　　　　　As yesterday!—ah, woe is me!

BOTH.　Oh, bury, bury—let the grave close o'er, etc.

Re-enter from the Ducal Palace the DUKE *and* DUCHESS, *followed by* DON ALHAMBRA DEL BOLERO, *the Grand Inquisitor.*

DUKE. My child, allow me to present to you His Distinction Don Alhambra del Bolero, the Grand Inquisitor of Spain. It was His Distinction who so thoughtfully abstracted your infant husband and brought him to Venice.

DON AL. So this is the little lady who is so unexpectedly called upon to assume the functions of Royalty! And a very nice little lady, too!

DUKE. Jimp, isn't she?

DON AL. Distinctly jimp. Allow me! (*Offers his hand. She turns away scornfully.*) Naughty temper!

DUKE. You must make some allowance. Her Majesty's head is a little turned by her access of dignity.

DON AL. I could have wished that Her Majesty's access of dignity had turned it in this direction.

DUCH. Unfortunately, if I am not mistaken, there appears to be some little doubt as to His Majesty's whereabouts.

CAS. (*aside*). A doubt as to his whereabouts? Then we may yet be saved!

DON AL. A doubt? Oh dear, no—no doubt at all! He is here, in Venice, plying the modest but picturesque calling of a gondolier. I can give you his address—I see him every day! In the entire annals of our history there is absolutely no circumstance so entirely free from all manner of doubt of any kind whatever! Listen, and I'll tell you all about it.

SONG—DON ALHAMBRA
(*with* DUKE, DUCHESS, CASILDA, *and* LUIZ)

I stole the Prince, and brought him here,
　　And left him gaily prattling
With a highly respectable gondolier,
Who promised the Royal babe to rear,
And teach him the trade of a timoneer
　　With his own beloved bratling.

Both of the babes were strong and stout,
   And, considering all things, clever.
Of that there is no manner of doubt—
No probable, possible shadow of doubt—
   No possible doubt whatever.

But owing, I'm much disposed to fear,
   To his terrible taste for tippling,
That highly respectable gondolier
Could never declare with a mind sincere
Which of the two was his offspring dear,
   And which the Royal stripling!

    Which was which he could never make out
      Despite his best endeavour.
    Of *that* there is no manner of doubt—
    No probable, possible shadow of doubt—
      No possible doubt whatever.

Time sped, and when at the end of a year
   I sought that infant cherished,
That highly respectable gondolier
Was lying a corpse on his humble bier—
I dropped a Grand Inquisitor's tear—
   That gondolier had perished.

    A taste for drink combined with gout,
      Had doubled him up for ever.
    Of *that* there is no manner of doubt—
    No probable, possible shadow of doubt—
      No possible doubt whatever.

The children followed his old career—
   (This statement can't be parried)
Of a highly respectable gondolier:
Well, one of the two (who will soon be here)—
But *which* of the two is not quite clear—
   Is the Royal Prince you married!

    Search in and out and round about,
      And you'll discover never
    A tale so free from every doubt—
    All probable, possible shadow of doubt—
      All possible doubt whatever!

CAS. Then do you mean to say that I am married to one of two gondoliers, but it is impossible to say which?

DON AL. Without any doubt of any kind whatever. But be reassured: the nurse to whom your husband was entrusted is the mother of the musical young man who is such a past-master of that delicately modulated instrument (*indicating the drum*). She can, no doubt, establish the King's identity beyond all question.

LUIZ. Heavens, how did he know that?

DON AL. My young friend, a Grand Inquisitor is always up to date. (*To* CAS.) His mother is at present the wife of a highly respectable and old-established brigand, who carries on an extensive practice in the mountains around Cordova. Accom-panied by two of my emissaries, he will set off at once for his mother's address. She will return with them, and if she finds any difficulty in making up her mind, the persuasive influence of the torture chamber will jog her memory.

RECITATIVE—CASILDA *and* DON ALHAMBRA

CAS.   But, bless my heart, consider my position!
      I am the wife of one, that's very clear;
      But who can tell, except by intuition,
         Which is the Prince, and which the Gondolier?

DON AL.   Submit to Fate without unseemly wrangle:
      Such complications frequently occur—
      Life is one closely complicated tangle:
         Death is the only true unraveller!

QUINTETTE—DUKE, DUCHESS, CASILDA, LUIZ,
and DON ALHAMBRA

ALL.   Try we life-long, we can never
      Straighten out life's tangled skein,
    Why should we, in vain endeavor,
      Guess and guess and guess again?

LUIZ.   Life's a pudding full of plums,

DUCH.   Care's a canker that benumbs.

ALL.   Life's a pudding full of plums,
      Care's a canker that benumbs.
   Wherefore waste our elocution
   On impossible solution?
   Life's a pleasant institution,
      Let us take it as it comes!

   Set aside the dull enigma,
      We shall guess it all too soon;
   Failure brings no kind of stigma—
      Dance we to another tune!

LUIZ.   String the lyre and fill the cup,

DUCH.   Lest on sorrow we should sup.

ALL.   String the lyre and fill the cup,
      Lest on sorrow we should sup.
   Hop and skip to Fancy's fiddle,
   Hands across and down the middle—
   Life's perhaps the only riddle
      That we shrink from giving up!

[*Exeunt all into Ducal Palace except* LUIZ, *who goes off in gondola.*

Enter Gondoliers and Contadine, followed by MARCO,
GIANETTA, GIUSEPPE, *and* TESSA

CHORUS

Bridegroom and bride!
   Knot that's insoluble,
   Voices all voluble

Hail it with pride.
Bridegroom and bride!
　　We in sincerity
　　Wish you prosperity,
Bridegroom and bride!

SONG—TESSA

TESS.　　When a merry maiden marries,
Sorrow goes and pleasure tarries;
　　Every sound becomes a song,
　　All is right, and nothing's wrong!
From to-day and ever after
Let our tears be tears of laughter.
　　Every sigh that finds a vent
　　Be a sigh of sweet content!
When you marry, merry maiden,
Then the air with love is laden;
　　Every flower is a rose,
　　　Every goose becomes a swan,
　　Every kind of trouble goes
　　　Where the last year's snows have gone

CHORUS.　Sunlight takes the place of shade
　　When you marry, merry maid!

TESS.　　When a merry maiden marries,
Sorrow goes and pleasure tarries;
　　Every sound becomes a song,
　　All is right, and nothing's wrong.
Gnawing Care and aching Sorrow,
Get ye gone until to-morrow;
　　Jealousies in grim array,
　　Ye are things of yesterday!
When you marry, merry maiden,
Then the air with joy is laden;
　　All the corners of the earth
　　　Ring with music sweetly played,
　　Worry is melodious mirth,
　　Grief is joy in masquerade;

CHORUS.　Sullen night is laughing day—
　　All the year is merry May!

At the end of the song, DON ALHAMBRA *enters at back. The Gondoliers and Contadine shrink from him, and gradually go off, much alarmed.*

GIU. And now our lives are going to begin in real earnest! What's a bachelor? A mere nothing—he's a chrysalis. He can't be said to live—he exists.

MAR. What a delightful institution marriage is! Why have we wasted all this time? Why didn't we marry ten years ago?

TESS. Because you couldn't find anybody nice enough.

GIA. Because you were waiting for *us*.

MAR. I suppose that *was* the reason. We were waiting for you without knowing it. (DON ALHAMBRA *comes forward.*) Hallo!

DON AL. Good morning.

GIU. If this gentleman is an undertaker it's a bad omen.

DON AL. Ceremony of some sort going on?

GIU. (*aside*). He *is* an undertaker! (*Aloud.*) No—a little unimportant family gathering. Nothing in *your* line.

DON AL. Somebody's birthday, I suppose?

GIA. Yes, mine!

TESS. And mine!

MAR. And mine!

GIU. And mine!

DON AL. Curious coincidence! And how old may you all be?

TESS. It's a rude question—but about ten minutes.

DON AL. Remarkably fine children! But surely you are jesting?

TESS. In other words, we were married about ten minutes since.

DON AL. Married! You don't mean to say you are married?

MAR. Oh yes, we were married.

DON AL. What, both of you?

ALL. All four of us.

DON AL. (*aside*). Bless my heart, how extremely awkward!

GIA. You don't mind, I suppose?

TESS. You were not thinking of either of us for yourself, I presume? Oh, Giuseppe, look at him—he was. He's heart-broken!

DON AL. No, no, I wasn't! I wasn't!

GIU. Now, my man (*slapping him on the back*), we don't want anything in your line to-day, and if your curiosity's satisfied—you can go!

DON AL. You mustn't call me your man. It's a liberty. I don't think you know who I am.

GIU. Not we, indeed! We are jolly gondoliers, the sons of Baptisto Palmieri, who led the last revolution. Republicans, heart and soul, we hold all men to be equal. As we abhor oppression, we abhor kings: as we detest vain-glory, we detest rank: as we despise effeminacy, we despise wealth. We are Venetian gondoliers—your equals in everything except our calling, and in that at once your masters and your servants.

DON AL. Bless my heart, how unfortunate! One of you may be Baptisto's son, for anything I know to the contrary; but the other is no less a personage than the only son of the late King of Barataria.

ALL. What!

DON AL. And I trust—I *trust* it was that one who slapped me on the shoulder and called me his man!

GIU. One of us a king!
MAR. Not brothers!
TESS. The King of Barataria!　　　} *Together.*
GIA. Well, who'd have thought it!
MAR. But which is it?

DON AL. What does it matter? As you are both Republicans, and hold kings in detestation, of course you'll abdicate at once. Good morning! (*Going.*)

GIA. *and* TESS. Oh, don't do that! (MARCO *and* GIUSEPPE *stop him.*)

GIU. Well, as to that, of course there are kings and kings. When I say that I detest kings, I mean I detest *bad* kings.

DON AL. I see. It's a delicate distinction.

GIU. Quite so. Now I can conceive a kind of king—an ideal king—the creature of my fancy, you know—who would be absolutely unobjectionable. A king, for instance, who would abolish taxes and make everything cheap, except gondolas—

MAR. And give a great many free entertainments to the gondoliers—

GIU. And let off fireworks on the Grand Canal, and engage all the gondolas for the occasion—

MAR. And scramble money on the Rialto among the gondoliers.

GIU. Such a king would be a blessing to his people, and if I were a king, that is the sort of king I would be.

MAR. And so would I!

DON AL. Come, I'm glad to find your objections are not insuperable.

MAR. *and* GIU. Oh, they're not insuperable.

GIA. *and* TESS. No, they're not insuperable.

GIU. Besides, we are open to conviction.

GIA. Yes; they are open to conviction.

TESS. Oh! they've often been convicted.

GIU. Our views may have been hastily formed on insufficient grounds. They may be crude, ill-digested, erroneous. I've a very poor opinion of the politican who is not open to conviction.

TESS. (*to* GIA.). Oh, he's a fine fellow!

GIA. Yes, that's the sort of politician for *my* money!

DON AL. Then we'll consider it settled. Now, as the country is in a state of insurrection, it is absolutely necessary that you should assume the reins of Government at once; and, until it is ascertained which of you is to be king, I have arranged that you will reign jointly, so that no question can arise hereafter as to the validity of any of your acts.

MAR. As one individual?

DON AL. As one individual.

GIU. (*linking himself with* MARCO). Like this?

DON AL. Something like that.

MAR. And we may take our friends with us, and give them places about the Court?

DON AL. Undoubtedly. That's always done!

MAR. I'm convinced!

GIU. So am I!

TESS. Then the sooner we're off the better.

GIA. We'll just run home and pack up a few things (*going*)—

DON AL. Stop, stop—that won't do at all—ladies are not admitted.

ALL. What!

DON AL. Not admitted. Not at present. Afterwards, perhaps. We'll see.

GIU. Why, you don't mean to say you are going to separate us from our wives!

DON AL. (*aside*). This is very awkward! (*Aloud.*) Only for a time—a few months. After all, what is a few months?

TESS. But we've only been married half an hour! (*Weeps.*)

FINALE—ACT I
SONG—GIANETTA

Kind sir, you cannot have the heart
  Our lives to part
 From those to whom an hour ago
   We were united!
Before our flowing hopes you stem,
  Ah, look at them,
 And pause before you deal this blow,
   All uninvited!
You men can never understand
  That heart and hand
 Cannot be separated when
   We go a-yearning;
You see, you've only women's eyes
  To idolize
 And only women's hearts, poor men,
   To set *you* burning!
Ah me, you men will never understand
That woman's heart is one with woman's hand!

Some kind of charm you seem to find
  In womankind—
 Some source of unexplained delight
   (Unless you're jesting),
But what attracts you, I confess,
  I cannot guess,
 To me a woman's face is quite
   Uninteresting!
If from my sister I were torn
  It could be borne—
 I should, no doubt, be horrified,
   But I could bear it;—
But Marco's quite another thing—
  He is my King,
 He has my heart and none beside
   Shall ever share it!
Ah me, you men will never understand
That woman's heart is one with woman's hand!

RECITATIVE—DON ALHAMBRA

Do not give way to this uncalled-for grief,
Your separation will be very brief.
  To ascertain which is the King
   And which the other,
  To Barataria's Court I'll bring
   His foster-mother;
  Her former nurseling to declare
   She'll be delighted.
That settled, let each happy pair be reunited.

MAR., GIU., GIA., TESS.	Viva! His argument is strong! Viva! We'll not be parted long! Viva! It will be settled soon! Viva! Then comes our honeymoon!

[*Exit* DON ALHAMBRA.

QUARTETTE—MARCO, GIUSEPPE, GIANETTA, TESSA

GIA. Then one of us will be a Queen,
   And sit on a golden throne,
     With a crown instead,
     Of a hat on her head,
   And diamonds all her own!
   With a beautiful robe of gold and green,
   I've always understood;
     I wonder whether
     She'd wear a feather?
   I rather think she should!

ALL. Oh, 'tis a glorious thing, I ween,
   To be a regular Royal Queen!
   No half-and-half affair, I mean,
   But a right-down regular Royal Queen!

MAR. She'll drive about in a carriage and pair,
   With the King on her left-hand side,
     And a milk-white horse,
     As a matter of course,
   Whenever she wants to ride!
   With beautiful silver shoes to wear
   Upon her dainty feet;
     With endless stocks
     Of beautiful frocks
   And as much as she wants to eat!

ALL. Oh, 'tis a glorious thing, I ween, etc.

TESS. Whenever she condescends to walk,
   Be sure she'll shine at that,
     With her haughty stare
     And her nose in the air,
   Like a well-born aristocrat!
   At elegant high society talk
   She'll bear away the bell,
     With her "How de do?"
     And her "How are you?"
   And "I trust I see you well!"

ALL. Oh, 'tis a glorious thing, I ween, etc.

GIU. And noble lords will scrape and bow,
   And double themselves in two,
     And open their eyes
     In blank surprise
   At whatever she likes to do.
   And everybody will roundly vow
   She's fair as flowers in May,
     And say, "How clever!"

     At whatsoever
     She condescends to say!

ALL. Oh, 'tis a glorious thing, I ween,
   To be a regular Royal Queen!
   No half-and-half affair, I mean,
   But a right-down regular Royal Queen!

Enter Chorus of Gondoliers and Contadine

CHORUS

Now, pray, what is the cause of this remarkable hilarity?
 This sudden ebullition of unmitigated jollity?
Has anybody blessed you with a sample of his charity?
 Or have you been adopted by a gentleman of quality?

MAR. *and* GIU. Replying, we sing
     As one individual,
     As I find I'm a king,
     To my kingdom I bid you all.
   I'm aware you object
     To pavilions and palaces,
   But you'll find I respect
     Your Republican fallacies.

CHORUS. As they know we object
     To pavilions and palaces,
   How can they respect
     Our Republican fallacies?

MARCO *and* GIUSEPPE

MAR. For every one who feels inclined,
   Some post we undertake to find
   Congenial with his frame of mind—
     And all shall equal be.

GIU. The Chancellor in his peruke—
   The Earl, the Marquis, and the Dook,
   The Groom, the Butler, and the Cook—
     They all shall equal be.

MAR. The Aristocrat who banks with Coutts—
   The Aristocrat who hunts and shoots—
   The Aristocrat who cleans our boots—
     They all shall equal be!

GIU. The Noble Lord who rules the State—
   The Noble Lord who cleans the plate—

MAR. The Noble Lord who scrubs the grate—
     They all shall equal be!

GIU. The Lord High Bishop orthodox—
   The Lord High Coachman on the box—

MAR. The Lord High Vagabond in the stocks—
     They all shall equal be!

BOTH. For every one, etc.

    Sing high, sing low,

And noble lords will scrape and bow, / And double themselves in two, . .

Wherever they go,
    They all shall equal be!

CHORUS.   Sing high, sing low,
           Wherever they go,
              They all shall equal be!

The Earl, the Marquis, and the Dook,
The Groom, the Butler, and the Cook,
The Aristocrat who banks with Coutts,
The Aristocrat who cleans the boots,
The Noble Lord who rules the State,
The Noble Lord who scrubs the grate,
The Lord High Bishop orthodox,
The Lord High Vagabond in the stocks—

For every one, etc.

        Sing high, sing low,
          Wherever they go,
            They all shall equal be!

        Then hail! O King,
          Whichever you may be,
        To you we sing,
          But do not bend the knee.
        Then hail! O King.

MARCO *and* GIUSEPPE (*together*)

Come, let's away—our island crown awaits me—
    Conflicting feelings rend my soul apart!
The thought of Royal dignity elates me,
    But leaving thee behind me breaks my heart!

(*Addressing* GIANETTA *and* TESSA.)

GIANETTA *and* TESSA (*together*)

Farewell, my love; on board you must be getting;
    But while upon the sea you gaily roam,
Remember that a heart for thee is fretting—
    The tender little heart you've left at home!

GIA.   Now, Marco dear,
        My wishes hear:
          While you're away
        It's understood
        You will be good,
          And not too gay.
        To every trace
        Of maiden grace
          You will be blind,
        And will not glance
        By any chance
          On womankind!

        If you are wise,
        You'll shut your eyes
          Till we arrive,
        And not address

        A lady less
          Than forty-five.
        You'll please to frown
        On every gown
          That you may see;
        And, O my pet,
        You won't forget
          You've married me!

And O my darling, O my pet,
Whatever else you may forget
In yonder isle beyond the sea,
Do not forget you've married me!

TESS.   You'll lay your head
        Upon your bed
          At set of sun.
        You will not sing
        Of anything
          To any one.
        You'll sit and mope
        All day, I hope,
          And shed a tear
        Upon the life
        Your little wife
          Is passing here.

        And if so be
        You think of me,
          Please tell the moon!
        I'll read it all
        In rays that fall
          On the lagoon:
        You'll be so kind
        As tell the wind
          How you may be,
        And send me words
        By little birds
          To comfort me!

And O my darling, O my pet,
Whatever else you may forget,
In yonder isle beyond the sea,
Do not forget you've married me!

QUARTETTE. Oh, my darling, O my pet, etc.

CHORUS (*during which a "Xebeque" is hauled
             alongside a quay*)

Then away we go to an island fair
    That lies in a Southern sea:
We know not where, and we don't much care,
    Wherever that isle may be.

THE MEN (*hauling on boat*).
           One, two, three,
              Haul!
           One, two, three,
              Haul!

One, two, three,
Haul!
With a will!

ALL. When the breezes are a-blowing
The ship will be going,
    When they don't we shall all stand still!
Then away we go to an island fair,
We know not where, and we don't much care,
    Wherever that isle may be.

SOLO—MARCO

Away we go
To a balmy isle,
Where the roses blow
All the winter while.

ALL (*hoisting sail*).

Then away we go to an island fair
That lies in a Southern sea:
Then away we go to an island fair,
Then away, then away, then away!

[*The men embark on the "Xebeque." MARCO and GIUSEPPE embracing GIANETTA and TESSA. The girls wave a farewell to the men as the curtain falls.*]

END OF ACT I

ACT II

SCENE.—*Pavilion in the Court of Barataria. MARCO and GIU-SEPPE, magnificently dressed, are seated on two thrones, oc-cupied in cleaning the crown and the sceptre. The Gondoliers are discovered, dressed, some as courtiers, officers of rank, etc., and others as private soldiers and servants of various degrees. All are enjoying themselves without reference to social distinc-tions—some playing cards, others throwing dice, some reading, others playing cup and ball, "morra," etc.*

CHORUS OF MEN *with* MARCO *and* GIUSEPPE

Of happiness the very pith
        In Barataria you may see:
A monarchy that's tempered with
        Republican Equality.
This form of government we find
The beau-ideal of its kind—
A despotism strict combined
        With absolute equality!

MARCO *and* GIUSEPPE

Two kings, of undue pride bereft,
        Who act in perfect unity,
Whom you can order right and left
        With absolute impunity.
Who put their subjects at their ease
By doing all they can to please!
And thus, to earn their bread-and-cheese,
        Seize every opportunity.

CHORUS. Of happiness, the very pith, etc.

MAR. Gentlemen, we are much obliged to you for your expressions of satisfaction and good feeling—I say, we are much obliged to you for your expressions of satisfaction and good feeling.

ALL. We heard you.

MAR. We are delighted, at any time, to fall in with senti-ments so charmingly expressed.

ALL. That's all right.

GIU. At the same time there is just one little grievance that we should like to ventilate.

ALL (*angrily*). What?

GIU. Don't be alarmed—it's not serious. It is arranged that, until it is decided which of us two is the actual King, we are to act as one person.

GIORGIO. Exactly.

GIU. Now, although we act as *one* person, we are, in point of fact, *two* persons.

ANNI. Ah, I don't think we can go into that. It is a legal fiction, and legal fictions are solemn things. Situated as we are, we can't recognize two independent responsibilities.

GIU. No; but you can recognize two independent appetites. It's all very well to say we act as one person, but when you supply us with only one ration between us, I should describe it as a legal fiction carried a little too far.

ANNI. It's rather a nice point. I don't like to express an opinion off-hand. Suppose we reserve it for argument before the full Court?

MAR. Yes, but what are we to do in the meantime?

MAR. *and* GIU. We want our tea.

ANNI. I think we may make an interim order for double rations on their Majesties entering into the usual undertaking to indemnify in the event of an adverse decision?

GIOR. That, I think, will meet the case. But you must work hard—stick to it—nothing like work.

GIU. Oh, certainly. We quite understand that a man who holds the magnificent position of King should do something to justify it. We are called "Your Majesty," we are allowed to buy ourselves magnificent clothes, our subjects frequently nod to us in the streets, the sentries always return our salutes, and we enjoy the inestimable privilege of heading the subscription lists to all the principal charities. In return for these advan-tages the least we can do is to make ourselves useful about the Palace.

SONG—GIUSEPPE *with* CHORUS

Rising early in the morning,
    We proceed to light the fire,
Then our Majesty adorning
    In its workaday attire,
        We embark without delay
        On the duties of the day.

First, we polish off some batches
Of political despatches,
    And foreign politicians circumvent:
Then, if business isn't heavy,
We may hold a Royal *levée*,
    Or ratify some Acts of Parliament.
Then we probably review the household troops—
With the usual "Shalloo humps!" and "Shalloo hoops!"
Or receive with ceremonial and state
An interesting Eastern potentate.
    After that we generally
    Go and dress our private *valet*—
(It's a rather nervous duty—he's a touchy little man)—
    Write some letters literary
    For our private secretary—
He is shaky in his spelling, so we help him if we can.
    Then, in view of cravings inner,
    We go down and order dinner;
Then we polish the Regalia and the Coronation Plate—
    Spend an hour in titivating
    All our Gentlemen-in-Waiting;
Or we run on little errands for the Ministers of State.

    Oh, philosophers may sing
    Of the troubles of a King;
Yet the duties are delightful, and the privileges great;
    But the privilege and pleasure
    That we treasure beyond measure
Is to run on little errands for the Ministers of State.

CHORUS. Oh, philosophers may sing, etc.

After luncheon (making merry
On a bun and glass of sherry),
    If we've nothing in particular to do,
We may make a Proclamation,
Or receive a deputation—
    Then we possibly create a Peer or two.
Then we help a fellow-creature on his path
With the Garter or the Thistle or the Bath
Or we dress and toddle off in semi-state
To a festival, a function, or a *fête*.
    Then we go and stand as sentry
    At the Palace (private entry),
Marching hither, marching thither, up and down and to and
        fro,
    While the warrior on duty
    Goes in search of beer and beauty

(And it generally happens that he hasn't far to go).
    He relieves us, if he's able,
    Just in time to lay the table,
Then we dine and serve the coffee, and at half-past twelve or
        one,
    With a pleasure that's emphatic,
    We retire to our attic
With the gratifying feeling that our duty has been done!

    Oh, philosophers may sing
    Of the troubles of a King;
But of pleasures there are many and of worries there are none;
    And the culminating pleasure
    That we treasure beyond measure
Is the gratifying feeling that our duty has been done!

CHORUS. Oh, philosophers may sing, etc.
                    [*Exeunt all but* MARCO *and* GIUSEPPE.

GIU. Yes, it really is a very pleasant existence. They're all so
singularly kind and considerate. You don't find them wanting
to do this, or wanting to do that, or saying "It's my turn
now." No, they let us have all the fun to ourselves, and never
seem to grudge it.

MAR. It makes one feel quite selfish. It almost seems like
taking advantage of their good nature.

GIU. How nice they were about the double rations.

MAR. Most considerate. Ah! there's only one thing wanting
to make us thoroughly comfortable.

GIU. And that is?

MAR. The dear little wives we left behind us three months
ago.

GIU. Yes, it *is* dull without female society. We can do
without everything else, but we can't do without that.

MAR. And if we have that in perfection, we have everything. There is only one recipe for perfect happiness.

SONG—MARCO

Take a pair of sparkling eyes,
    Hidden, ever and anon,
        In a merciful eclipse—
Do not heed their mild surprise—
    Having passed the Rubicon,
        Take a pair of rosy lips;
Take a figure trimly planned—
    Such as admiration whets
        (Be particular in this);
Take a tender little hand,
    Fringed with dainty fingerettes,
        Press it—in parenthesis;—
Ah! Take all these, you lucky man—
Take and keep them, if you can!

Take a pretty little cot—
    Quite a miniature affair—
        Hung about with trellised vine,

Furnish it upon the spot
  With the treasures rich and rare
   I've endeavoured to define.
Live to love and love to live—
  You will ripen at your ease,
   Growing on the sunny side—
Fate has nothing more to give.
  You're a dainty man to please
   If you are not satisfied.
Ah! Take my counsel, happy man;
Act upon it, if you can!

Enter Chorus of Contadine, running in, led by FIAMETTA *and*
VITTORIA. *They are met by all the Ex-Gondoliers, who welcome them heartily.*

SCENA—CHORUS OF GIRLS, QUARTETTE, DUET *and* CHORUS

 Here we are, at the risk of our lives,
 From ever so far, and we've brought your wives—
 And to that end we've crossed the main,
 And don't intend to return again!

FIA.   Though obedience is strong,
     Curiosity's stronger—
   We waited for long,
     Till we couldn't wait longer.

VIT.   It's imprudent, we know,
     But without your society
   Existence was slow,
     And we wanted variety—

ALL. So here we are, at the risk of our lives,
  From ever so far, and we've brought your wives—
  And to that end we've crossed the main,
  And don't intend to return again!

Enter GIANETTA *and* TESSA. *They rush to the arms
of* MARCO *and* GIUSEPPE

GIU. Tessa!
TESS.   Giuseppe! ⎫
GIA. Marco!   ⎬ *Embrace.*
MAR.   Gianetta! ⎭

TESSA *and* GIANETTA

TESS. After sailing to this island—
GIA.   Tossing in a manner frightful,
TESS. We are all once more on dry land—
GIA.   And we find the change delightful,
TESS. As at home we've been remaining—
   We've not seen you both for ages,
GIA. Tell me, are you fond of reigning?—
   How's the food, and what's the wages?
TESS. Does your new employment please ye?—
GIA.   How does Royalizing strike you?
TESS. Is it difficult or easy?—
GIA.   Do you think your subjects like you?

TESS. I am anxious to elicit,
   Is it plain and easy steering?
GIA. Take it altogether, is it—
   Better fun than gondoliering?
BOTH. We shall both go on requesting
   Till you tell us, never doubt it;
  Everything is interesting,
   Tell us, tell us all about it!

CHORUS. They will both go on requesting, etc.

TESS. Is the populace exacting?
GIA.   Do they keep you at a distance?
TESS. All unaided are you acting,
GIA.   Or do they provide assistance?
TESS. When you're busy, have you got to
   Get up early in the morning?
GIA. If you do what you ought not to,
   Do they give the usual warning?
TESS. With a horse do they equip you?
GIA.   Lots of trumpeting and drumming?
TESS. Do the Royal tradesmen tip you?
GIA.   Ain't the livery becoming!
TESS. Does your human being inner
   Feed on everything that nice is?
GIA. Do they give you wine for dinner;
   Peaches, sugar-plums, and ices?
BOTH. We shall both go on requesting
   Till you tell us, never doubt it;
  Everything is interesting,
   Tell us, tell us all about it!

CHORUS. They will both go on requesting, etc.

MAR. This is indeed a most delightful surprise!

TESS. Yes, we thought you'd like it. You see, it was like this. After you left we felt very dull and mopey, and the days crawled by, and you never wrote; so at last I said to Gianetta, "I can't stand this any longer; those two poor Monarchs haven't got any one to mend their stockings or sew on their buttons or patch their clothes—at least, I hope they haven't—let us all pack up a change and go and see how they're getting on." And she said, "Done," and they all said, "Done"; and we asked old Giacopo to lend us his boat, and *he* said, "Done"; and we've crossed the sea, and, thank goodness, *that's* done; and here we are, and—and—*I've* done!

GIA. And now—which of you is King?

TESS. And which of us is Queen?

GIU. That we shan't know until Nurse turns up. But never mind that—the question is, how shall we celebrate the commencement of our honeymoon? Gentlemen, will you allow us to offer you a magnificent banquet?

ALL. We will!

GIU. Thanks very much; and, ladies, what do you say to a dance?

TESS. A banquet *and* a dance! O, it's too much happiness!

CHORUS *and* DANCE

Dance a cachucha, fandango, bolero,
Xeres we'll drink—Manzanilla, Montero—
Wine, when it runs in abundance, enhances
The reckless delight of that wildest of dances!
        To the pretty pitter-pitter-patter,
        And the clitter-clitter-clitter-clatter—
            Clitter—clitter—clatter,
            Pitter—pitter—patter,
        Patter, patter, patter, patter, we'll dance.
    Old Xeres we'll drink—Manzanilla, Montero;
    For wine, when it runs in abundance, enhances
    The reckless delight of that wildest of dances!

(*Cachucha*)

The dance is interrupted by the unexpected appearance of DON
ALHAMBRA, *who looks on with astonishment.* MARCO *and*
GIUSEPPE *appear embarrassed. The others run off, except
Drummer Boy, who is driven off by* DON ALHAMBRA.

DON AL. Good evening. Fancy ball?

GIU. No, not exactly. A little friendly dance. That's all.
Sorry you're late.

DON AL. But I saw a groom dancing, and a footman!

MAR. Yes. That's the Lord High Footman.

DON AL. And, dear me, a common little drummer boy!

GIU. Oh no! That's the Lord High Drummer Boy.

DON AL. But surely, surely the servants'-hall is the place for
these gentry?

GIU. Oh dear no! *We* have appropriated the servants'-hall.
It's the Royal Apartment, and accessible only by tickets ob-
tainable at the Lord Chamberlain's office.

MAR. We really must have some place that we can call our
own.

DON AL. (*puzzled*). I'm afraid I'm not quite equal to the
intellectual pressure of the conversation.

GIU. You see, the Monarchy has been re-modelled on Re-
publican principles.

DON AL. What!

GIU. All departments rank equally, and everybody is at the
head of his department.

DON AL. I see.

MAR. I'm afraid you're annoyed.

DON AL. No. I won't say that. It's not quite what I
expected.

GIU. I'm awfully sorry.

MAR. So am I.

GIU. By the by, can I offer you anything after your voyage?
A plate of macaroni and a rusk?

DON AL. (*preoccupied*). No, no—nothing—nothing.

GIU. Obliged to be careful?

DON AL. Yes—gout. You see, in every Court there are dis-
tinctions that must be observed.

GIU. (*puzzled*). There are, are there?

DON AL. Why, of course. For instance, you wouldn't have a

Lord High Chancellor play leapfrog with his own cook.

MAR. Why not?

DON AL. Why not! Because a Lord High Chancellor is a
personage of great dignity, who should never, under any circumstances, place himself in the position of being told to
tuck in his tuppenny, except by noblemen of his own rank. A
Lord High Archbishop, for instance, might tell a Lord High
Chancellor to tuck in his tuppenny, but certainly not a cook,
gentlemen, certainly not a cook.

GIU. Not even a Lord High Cook?

DON AL. My good friend, that is a rank that is not recog-
nized at the Lord Chamberlain's office. No, no, it won't do.
I'll give you an instance in which the experiment was tried.

SONG—DON ALHAMBRA, *with* MARCO *and* GIUSEPPE

DON AL.   There lived a King, as I've been told,
            In the wonder-working days of old,
            When hearts were twice as good as gold,
                And twenty times as mellow.
            Good-temper triumphed in his face,
            And in his heart he found a place
            For all the erring human race
                And every wretched fellow.
            When he had Rhenish wine to drink
            It made him very sad to think
            That some, at junket or at jink,
                Must be content with toddy.

MAR. *and* GIU. With toddy, must be content with toddy.

DON AL.   He wished all men as rich as he
            (And he was rich as rich could be),
            So to the top of every tree
                Promoted everybody.

MAR. *and* GIU. Now, that's the kind of King for me—
            He wished all men as rich as he,
            So to the top of every tree
                Promoted everybody!

DON AL.   Lord Chancellors were cheap as sprats,
            And Bishops in their shovel hats
            Were plentiful as tabby cats—
                In point of fact, too many.
            Ambassadors cropped up like hay,
            Prime Ministers and such as they
            Grew like asparagus in May,
                And Dukes were three a penny.
            On every side Field-Marshals gleamed,
            Small beer were Lords-Lieutenant deemed,
            With Admirals the ocean teemed
                All round his wide dominions.

MAR. *and* GIU. With Admirals all round his wide dominions.

DON AL.   And Party Leaders you might meet
            In twos and threes in every street

I was always very wary, / For his fury was ecstatic—

> Maintaining, with no little heat,
> Their various opinions.

MAR. *and* CIU.
> Now that's a sight you couldn't beat—
> Two Party Leaders in each street
> Maintaining, with no little heat,
> Their various opinions.

DON AL.
> That King, although no one denies
> His heart was of abnormal size,
> Yet he'd have acted otherwise
> If he had been acuter.
> The end is easily foretold,
> When every blessed thing you hold
> Is made of silver, or of gold,
> You long for simple pewter.
> When you have nothing else to wear
> But cloth of gold and satins rare,
> For cloth of gold you cease to care—
> Up goes the price of shoddy.

MAR. *and* GIU.
> Of shoddy, up goes the price of shoddy.

DON AL.
> In short, whoever you may be,
> To this conclusion you'll agree,
> When every one is somebodee,
> Then no one's anybody!

MAR. *and* GIU.
> Now that's as plain as plain can be,
> To this conclusion we agree—

ALL.
> When every one is somebodee,
> Then no one's anybody!

GIANETTA *and* TESSA *enter unobserved. The two girls, impelled by curiosity, remain listening at the back of the stage.*

DON AL. And now I have some important news to communicate. His Grace the Duke of Plaza-Toro, Her Grace the Duchess, and their beautiful daughter Casilda—I say their beautiful daughter Casilda—

GIU. We heard you.

DON AL. Have arrived at Barataria, and may be here at any moment.

MAR. The Duke and Duchess are nothing to us.

DON AL. But the daughter—the beautiful daughter! Aha! Oh, you're a lucky dog, one of you!

GIU. I think you're a very incomprehensible old gentleman.

DON AL. Not a bit—I'll explain. Many years ago when you (whichever you are) were a baby, you (whichever you are) were married to a little girl who has grown up to be the most beautiful young lady in Spain. That beautiful young lady will be here to claim you (whichever you are) in half an hour, and I congratulate that one (whichever it is) with all my heart.

MAR. Married when a baby!

GIU. But we were married three months ago!

DON AL. One of you—only one. The other (whichever it is) is an unintentional bigamist.

GIA. *and* TESS. (*coming forward*). Well, upon my word!

DON AL. Eh? Who are these young people?

TESS. Who are we? Why, their wives, of course. We've just arrived.

DON AL. Their wives! Oh dear, this is very unfortunate! Oh dear, this complicates matters! Dear, dear, what will Her Majesty say?

GIA. And do you mean to say that one of these Monarchs was already married?

TESS. And that neither of us will be a Queen?

DON AL. That is the idea I intended to convey. (TESSA *and* GIANETTA *begin to cry.*)

GIU. (*to* TESSA). Tessa, my dear, dear child—

TESS. Get away! perhaps it's you!

MAR. (*to* GIA.). My poor, poor little woman!

GIA. Don't! Who knows whose husband you are?

TESS. And pray, why didn't you tell us all about it before they left Venice?

DON AL. Because, if I had, no earthly temptation would have induced these gentlemen to leave two such extremely fascinating and utterly irresistible little ladies!

TESS. There's something in that.

DON AL. I may mention that you will not be kept long in suspense, as the old lady who nursed the Royal child is at present in the torture chamber, waiting for me to interview her.

GIU. Poor old girl. Hadn't you better go and put her out of her suspense?

DON AL. Oh no—there's no hurry—she's all right. She has all the illustrated papers. However, I'll go and interrogate her, and, in the meantime, may I suggest the absolute propriety of your regarding yourselves as single young ladies. Good evening!

> [*Exit* DON ALHAMBRA.

GIA. Well, here's a pleasant state of things!

MAR. Delightful. One of us is married to two young ladies, and nobody knows which; and the other is married to one young lady whom nobody can identify!

GIA. And one of us is married to one of you, and the other is married to nobody.

TESS. But which of you is married to which of us, and what's to become of the other? (*About to cry.*)

GIA. It's quite simple. Observe. Two husbands have managed to acquire three wives. Three wives—two husbands. (*Reckoning up.*) That's two-thirds of a husband to each wife.

TESS. O Mount Vesuvius, here we are in arithmetic! My good sir, one can't marry a vulgar fraction!

GIU. You've no right to call me a vulgar fraction.

MAR. We are getting rather mixed. The situation is entangled. Let's try and comb it out.

QUARTETTE—MARCO, GIUSEPPE, GIANETTA, TESSA

> In a contemplative fashion,
> And a tranquil frame of mind,
> Free from every kind of passion,
> Some solution let us find.

Let us grasp the situation,
    Solve the complicated plot—
Quiet, calm deliberation
    Disentangles every knot.

TESS. I, no doubt, Giuseppe wedded—
    That's, of course, a slice of luck.
He is rather dunder-headed,
    Still distinctly, he's a duck.

THE OTHERS. In a contemplative fashion, etc.

GIA. I, a victim, too, of Cupid,
    Marco married—that is clear.
He's particularly stupid,
    Still distinctly, he's a dear.

THE OTHERS. Let us grasp the situation, etc.

MAR. To Gianetta I was mated;
    I can prove it in a trice:
Though her charms are overrated,
    Still I own she's rather nice.

THE OTHERS. In a contemplative fashion, etc.

GIU. I to Tessa, willy-nilly,
    All at once a victim fell.
She is what is called a silly,
    Still she answers pretty well.

THE OTHERS. Let us grasp the situation, etc.

MAR.   Now when we were pretty babies
        Some one married us, that's clear—

GIA.   And if I can catch her
        I'll pinch her and scratch her,
  And send her away with a flea in her ear.

GIU.   He whom that young lady married,
        To receive her can't refuse.

TESS.   If I overtake her
      I'll warrant I'll make her
  To shake in her aristocratical shoes!

GIA. (*to* TESS.). If she married your Giuseppe
        You and he will have to part—

TESS. (*to* GIA.).   If I have to do it
      I'll warrant she'll rue it—
  I'll teach her to marry the man of my
        heart!

TESS. (*to* GIA.). If she married Messer Marco
        You're a spinster, that is plain—

GIA. (*to* TESS.).   No matter—no matter
      If I can get at her
  I doubt if her mother will know her
        again!

ALL.   Quiet, calm deliberation
       Disentangles every knot!

[Exeunt, pondering.

MARCH. *Enter procession of Retainers, heralding approach of* DUKE, DUCHESS, *and* CASILDA. *All three are now dressed with the utmost magnificence.*

CHORUS OF MEN, *with* DUKE *and* DUCHESS

With ducal pomp and ducal pride
    (Announce these comers,
      O ye kettle-drummers!)
Comes Barataria's high-born bride.
    (Ye sounding cymbals clang!)
She comes to claim the Royal hand—
    (Proclaim their Graces,
      O ye double basses!)
Of the King who rules this goodly land.
    (Ye brazen brasses bang!)

DUKE *and* This polite attention touches
DUCH.   Heart of Duke and heart of Duchess.
      Who resign their pet
      With profound regret.
   She of beauty was a model
   When a tiny tiddle-toddle,
      And at twenty-one
      She's excelled by none!

CHORUS.   With ducal pomp and ducal pride, etc.

DUKE (*to his attendants*). Be good enough to inform His Majesty that His Grace the Duke of Plaza-Toro, Limited, has arrived, and begs—

CAS. Desires—

DUCH. Demands—

DUKE. And demands an audience. (*Exeunt attendants.*) And now, my child, prepare to receive the husband to whom you were united under such interesting and romantic circumstances.

CAS. But which is it? There are two of them!

DUKE. It is true that at present His Majesty is a double gentleman; but as soon as the circumstances of his marriage are ascertained, he will, *ipso facto,* boil down to a single gentleman—thus presenting a unique example of an individual who becomes a single man and a married man by the same operation.

DUCH. (*severely*). I have known instances in which the characteristics of both conditions existed concurrently in the same individual.

DUKE. Ah, he couldn't have been a Plaza-Toro.

DUCH. Oh! couldn't he, though!

CAS. Well, whatever happens, I shall, of course, be a dutiful wife, but I can never love my husband.

DUKE. I don't know. It's extraordinary what unprepossessing people one can love if one give's one's mind to it.

DUCH. I loved your father.

DUKE. My love—that remark is a little hard, I think? Rather cruel, perhaps? Somewhat uncalled-for, I venture to believe?

DUCH. It was very difficult, my dear; but I said to myself, "That man is a Duke, and I *will* love him." Several of my relations bet me I couldn't, but I did—desperately!

SONG—DUCHESS

On the day when I was wedded
To your admirable sire,
I acknowledge that I dreaded
An explosion of his ire.
I was overcome with panic—
For his temper was volcanic,
And I didn't dare revolt,
For I feared a thunderbolt!
I was always very wary,
For his fury was ecstatic—
His refined vocabulary
Most unpleasantly emphatic.
To the thunder
Of this Tartar
I knocked under
Like a martyr;
When intently
He was fuming,
I was gently
Unassuming—
When reviling
Me completely,
I was smiling
Very sweetly:
Giving him the very best, and getting back the very worst—
That is how I tried to tame your great progenitor—at first!
But I found that a reliance
On my threatening appearance,
And a resolute defiance
Of marital interference,
And a gentle intimation
Of my firm determination
To see what I could do
To be wife and husband too
Was the only thing required
For to make his temper supple,
And you couldn't have desired
A more reciprocating couple.
Ever willing
To be wooing,
We were billing—
We were cooing;
When I merely
From him parted,
We were nearly
Broken-hearted—
When in sequel
Reunited,
We were equal-
Ly delighted.
So with double-shotted guns and colors nailed unto the mast,
I tamed your insignificant progenitor—at last!

CAS. My only hope is that when my husband sees what a

shady family he has married into he will repudiate the contract altogether.

DUKE. Shady? A nobleman shady, who is blazing in the lustre of unaccustomed pocket-money? A nobleman shady, who can look back upon ninety-five quarterings? It is not every nobleman who is ninety-five quarters in arrear—I mean, who can look back upon ninety-five of them! And this, just as I have been floated at a premium! Oh fie!

DUCH. Your Majesty is surely unaware that directly Your Majesty's father came before the public he was applied for over and over again.

DUKE. My dear, Her Majesty's father was in the habit of being applied for over and over again—and very urgently applied for, too—long before he was registered under the Limited Liability Act.

RECITATIVE—DUKE

To help unhappy commoners, and add to their enjoyment,
Affords a man of noble rank congenial employment;
Of our attempts we offer you examples illustrative:
The work is light, and, I may add, it's most remunerative.

DUET—DUKE *and* DUCHESS

DUKE   Small titles and orders
For Mayors and Recorders
I get—and they're highly delighted—

DUCH.   They're highly delighted!

DUKE.   M.P.'s baronetted,
Sham Colonels gazetted,
And second-rate Aldermen knighted—

DUCH.   Yes, Aldermen knighted.

DUKE.   Foundation-stone laying
I find very paying:
It adds a large sum to my makings—

DUCH.   Large sums to his makings.

DUKE.   At charity dinners
The best of speech-spinners,
I get ten per cent on the takings—

DUCH.   One-tenth of the takings.

DUCH.   I present any lady
Whose conduct is shady
Or smacking of doubtful propriety—

DUKE.   Doubtful propriety.

DUCH.   When Virtue would quash her,
I take and whitewash her,
And launch her in first-rate society—

DUKE.   First-rate society!

DUCH. I recommend acres
Of clumsy dressmakers–
   Their fit and their finishing touches–

DUKE.   Their finishing touches.

DUCH. A sum in addition
They pay for permission
   To say that they make for the Duchess–

DUKE.   They make for the Duchess!

DUKE. Those pressing prevailers,
The ready-made tailors,
   Quote me as their great double-barrel–

DUCH.   Their great double-barrel.

DUKE I allow them to do so,
Though Robinson Crusoe
   Would jib at their wearing apparel–

DUCH.   Such wearing apparel!

DUKE. I sit, by selection,
Upon the direction
   Of several Companies bubble–

DUCH.   All Companies bubble!

DUKE. As soon as they're floated,
I'm freely bank-noted–
   I'm pretty well paid for my trouble–

DUCH.   He's paid for his trouble!

DUCH. At middle-class party
I play at écarté–
   And I'm by no means a beginner–

DUKE (significantly). She's not a beginner.

DUCH. To one of my station
The remuneration–
   Five guineas a night and my dinner–

DUKE.   And wine with her dinner.

DUCH. I write letters blatant
On medicines patent–
   And use any other you mustn't–

DUKE.   Believe me, you mustn't–

DUCH. And vow my complexion
Derives its perfection
   From somebody's soap–which it doesn't–

DUKE (significantly). It certainly doesn't!

DUKE. We're ready as witness
To any one's fitness
   To fill any place or preferment–

DUCH.   A place or preferment.

DUCH. We're often in waiting
At junket or *fêting,*
   And sometimes attend an interment–

DUKE.   We enjoy an interment.

BOTH. In short, if you kindle
The spark of a swindle,
   Lure simpletons into your clutches–
   Yes; into your clutches.
Or hoodwink a debtor,
You cannot do better

DUCH.   Than trot out a Duke or a Duchess–

DUKE.   A Duke or a Duchess!

Enter MARCO *and* GIUSEPPE

DUKE. Ah! Their Majesties. Your Majesty! (*Bows with great ceremony.*)

MAR. The Duke of Plaza-Toro, I believe?

DUKE. The same. (MARCO *and* GIUSEPPE *offer to shake hands with him.* THE DUKE *bows ceremoniously. They endeavour to imitate him.*) Allow me to present–

GIU. The young lady one of us married?

(MARCO *and* GIUSEPPE *offer to shake hands with her.* CASILDA *curtsies formally. They endeavour to imitate her.*)

CAS. Gentlemen, I am the most obedient servant of one of you. (*Aside.*) Oh, Luiz!

DUKE. I am now about to address myself to the gentleman whom my daughter married; the other may allow his attention to wander if he likes, for what I am about to say does not concern him. Sir, you will find in this young lady a combination of excellences which you would search for in vain in any young lady who had not the good fortune to be my daughter. There is some little doubt as to which of you is the gentleman I am addressing, and which is the gentleman who is allowing his attention to wander; but when that doubt is solved, I shall say (still addressing the attentive gentleman), "Take her, and may she make you happier than her mother has made me."

DUCH. Sir!

DUKE. If possible. And now there is a little matter to which I think I am entitled to take exception. I come here in state with Her Grace the Duchess and Her Majesty my daughter, and what do I find? Do I find, for instance, a guard of honour to receive me? No!

MAR. *and* GIU. No.

DUKE. The town illuminated? No!

MAR. *and* GIU. No!

DUKE. Refreshment provided? No!

MAR. *and* GIU. No.

DUKE. A Royal salute fired? No!

MAR. *and* GIU. No.

DUKE. Triumphal arches erected? No!

MAR. *and* GIU. No.

DUKE. The bells set ringing?

MAR. *and* GIU. No.

DUKE. Yes—one—the Visitors', and I rang it myself. It is not enough! It is not enough!

GIU. Upon my honour, I'm very sorry; but you see, I was brought up in a gondola, and my ideas of politeness are confined to taking off my cap to my passengers when they tip me.

DUCH. That's all very well in its way, but it is not enough.

GIU. I'll take off anything else in reason.

DUKE. But a Royal Salute to my daughter—it costs so little.

CAS. Papa, I don't want a salute.

GIU. My dear sir, as soon as we know which of us is entitled to take that liberty she shall have as many salutes as she likes.

MAR. As for guards of honour and triumphal arches, you don't know our people—they wouldn't stand it.

GIU. They are very off-hand with us—very off-hand indeed.

DUKE. Oh, but you mustn't allow that—you must keep them in proper discipline, you must impress your Court with your importance. You want deportment—carriage—

GIU. We've got a carriage.

DUKE. Manner—dignity. There must be a good deal of this sort of thing—(*business*)—and a little of this sort of thing—(*business*)—and possibly just a *Soupçon* of this sort of thing!—(*business*)—and so on. Oh, it's very useful, and most effective. Just attend to me. You are a King—I am a subject. Very good—

(*Gavotte*)

DUKE, DUCHESS, CASILDA, MARCO, GIUSEPPE

DUKE.	I am a courtier grave and serious Who is about to kiss your hand: Try to combine a pose imperious With a demeanour nobly bland.
MAR. *and* GIU.	Let us combine a pose imperious With a demeanour nobly bland.

(MARCO *and* GIUSEPPE *endeavour to carry out his instructions.*)

DUKE.	That's, if anything, *too* unbending— Too aggressively stiff and grand;

(*They suddenly modify their attitudes.*)

	Now to the other extreme you're tending— Don't be so deucedly condescending!
DUCH. *and* CAS.	Now to the other extreme you're tending— Don't be so dreadfully condescending!
MAR. *and* GIU.	Oh, hard to please some noblemen seem! At first, if anything, *too* unbending; Off we go to the other extreme— Too confoundedly condescending!
DUKE.	Now a gavotte perform sedately—

	Offer your hand with conscious pride; Take an attitude not too stately, Still sufficiently dignified.
MAR. *and* GIU.	Now for an attitude not too stately, Still sufficiently dignified.

(*They endeavour to carry out his instructions.*)

DUKE (*beating time*).	Oncely, twicely—oncely, twicely— Bow impressively ere you glide.

(*They do so.*)

	Capital both—you've caught it nicely! That is the style of thing precisely!
DUCH. *and* CAS.	Capital both—they've caught it nicely! That is the style of thing precisely!
MAR. *and* GIU.	Oh, sweet to earn a nobleman's praise! Capital both—we've caught it nicely! Supposing he's right in what he says, This is the style of thing precisely!

[GAVOTTE. *At the end exeunt* DUKE *and* DUCHESS, *leaving* CASILDA *with* MARCO *and* GIUSEPPE.

GIU. (*to* MARCO). The old birds have gone away and left the young chickens together. That's called tact.

MAR. It's very awkward. We really ought to tell her how we are situated. It's not fair to the girl.

GIU. Then why don't you do it?

MAR. I'd rather not—you.

GIU. I don't know how to begin. (*To* CASILDA.) A—Madam—I—we, that is, several of us—

CAS. Gentlemen, I am bound to listen to you; but it is right to tell you that, not knowing I was married in infancy, I am over head and ears in love with somebody else.

GIU. Our case exactly! *We* are over head and ears in love with somebody else! (*Enter* GIANETTA *and* TESSA.) In point of fact, with our wives!

CAS. Your wives! Then you are married?

TESS. It's not our fault.

GIA. We knew nothing about it.

BOTH. We are sisters in misfortune.

CAS. My good girls, I don't blame you. Only before we go any further we must really arrive at some satisfactory arrangement, or we shall get hopelessly complicated.

QUINTETTE AND FINALE
MARCO, GIUSEPPE, CASILDA, GIANETTA, TESSA

ALL.	Here is a case unprecedented! Here are a King and Queen ill-starred! Ever since marriage was first invented Never was known a case so hard!
MAR. *and* GIU.	I may be said to have been bisected, By a profound catastrophe!

And a gentle intimation / Of my firm determination . . .

CAS., GIA., TESS.	Through a calamity unexpected I am divisible into three!
ALL.	O moralists all, How can you call Marriage a state of unitee, When excellent husbands are bisected, And wives divisible into three? O moralists all, How can you call Marriage a state of union true?
CAS., GIA., TESS.	One-third of myself is married to half of ye or you,
MAR. *and* GIU.	When half of myself has married one-third of ye or you?

Enter DON ALHAMBRA, *followed by* DUKE, DUCHESS, *and all the* CHORUS

FINALE

RECITATIVE—DON ALHAMBRA

Now let the loyal lieges gather round—
The Prince's foster-mother has been found!
She will declare, to silver clarion's sound,
The rightful King—let him forthwith be crowned!

CHORUS.	She will declare, etc.

[DON ALHAMBRA *brings forward* INEZ, *the Prince's foster-mother.*

TESS.	Speak, woman, speak—
DUKE.	We're all attention!
GIA.	The news we seek—
DUCH.	This moment mention.
CAS.	To us they bring—
DON AL.	His foster-mother.
MAR.	Is he the King?
GIU.	Or this my brother?
ALL.	Speak, woman, speak, etc.

RECITATIVE—INEZ

The Royal Prince was by the King entrusted
To my fond care, ere I grew old and crusted;
When traitors came to steal his son reputed,
My own small boy I deftly substituted!
The villains fell into the trap completely—
I hid the Prince away—still sleeping sweetly:
I called him "son" with pardonable slyness—
His name, Luiz! Behold his Royal Highness!

[*Sensation.* LUIZ *ascends the throne, crowned and robed as King.*

CAS. (*rushing to his arms*).	Luiz!
LUIZ.	Casilda! (*Embrace.*)
ALL.	Is this indeed the King? Oh, wondrous revelation! Oh, unexpected thing! Unlooked-for situation!
MAR., GIA., GIU., TESS.	This statement we receive With sentiments conflicting; Our hearts rejoice and grieve, Each other contradicting; To those whom we adore We can be reunited— On one point rather sore, But, on the whole, delighted!
LUIZ.	When others claimed thy dainty hand, I waited—waited—waited,
DUKE.	As prudence (so I understand) Dictated—tated—tated.
CAS.	By virtue of our early vow Recorded—corded—corded.
DUCH.	Your pure and patient love is now Rewarded—warded—warded.
ALL.	Then hail, O King of a Golden Land, And the high-born bride who claims his hand! The past is dead, and you gain your own, A royal crown and a golden throne!

[*All kneel:* LUIZ *crowns* CASILDA.

ALL.	Once more *gondolieri*, Both skilful and wary, Free from this quandary Contented are we. From Royalty flying, Our gondolas plying, And merrily crying Our "premé," "stalì!"

So good-bye, cachucha, fandango, bolero—
We'll dance a farewell to that measure—
Old Xeres, adieu—Manzanilla—Montero—
We leave you with feelings of pleasure!

CURTAIN